The Veda
Made Simple

The Veda
Made Simple

Pariksith Singh, MD

ink | kāli

Title: The Veda Made Simple
Author: Pariksith Singh

ISBN: 978-93-92209-51-2

First published in India 2023
This edition published 2023

Published by:
BluOne Ink LLP
A-76, 2nd Floor, Noida Sector 136,
Uttar Pradesh 201305

Website: www.bluone.ink
Email: publisher@bluone.ink

Printed in India at Nutech Print Services

Kali, Occam and BluPrint are all trademarks of BluOne Ink LLP.

"I seek not science, not religion, not Theosophy, but Veda – the truth about Brahman, not only about His essentiality, but about His manifestation, not a lamp on the way to the forest, but a light and a guide to joy and action in the world, the truth which is beyond opinion, the knowledge which all thought strives after – *yasmin vijiate sarvam vijiatam.* I believe that Veda to be the foundation of the Sanatan Dharma; I believe it to be the concealed divinity within Hinduism, but a veil has to be drawn aside, a curtain has to be lifted. I believe it to be knowable and discoverable. I believe the future of India and the world to depend on its discovery and on its application, not to the renunciation of life, but to life in the world and among men."

—**Sri Aurobindo,** *Essays Divine and Human*

Contents

IV *Yajna* and the Fourfold Godhead of the Veda

V The Invocation

Foreword

The *Rig Veda* is the oldest book in the world. It is like an ancient monument in pristine form for we know it was passed down without change of a single syllable by the use of mnemonic devices that have ensured perfect fidelity.

Its internal evidence, such as the mention that Sarasvati was the greatest river of its time, indicates memory of a period prior to 3,000 BCE. This is because the 3rd millennium BCE Harappan era settlements on the Sarasvati River extend only up to the desert in Rajasthan, suggesting that the river had ceased flowing to the ocean before this time. It also recalls astronomical events of the 4th millennium BCE and, most amazingly, its organization is according to a code which indicates that the Vedic rishis knew that the sun and the moon are about 108 times their diameter from the earth.

Our fascination for the *Rig Veda* is not only for historical and antiquarian reasons but also as a source of the deepest spiritual and psychological knowledge. The *Rig Veda* has been traditionally called *ātma-vidyā*, "science of consciousness", and as consciousness is the frontier of modern science, this ancient text has assumed renewed contemporary relevance.

Those who doubt that ancient wisdom could be useful to humanity now, when science has changed in fundamental ways in the last few centuries, must remember that all knowledge exists in the mind and therefore ancient sages in touch with their consciousness could have had insights that remain valuable. Academics who have looked at the *Rig Veda* from an anthropological lens have been led astray by the implicit assumptions of this approach in which consciousness emerges on the ground of materiality.

The *Rig Veda* is also indirectly relevant in addressing the pressing issue of our times, which is whether artificial intelligence machines of the future will attain consciousness. Should that happen, it is most likely that such machines will enslave, if not destroy, mankind.

My own take is that computers will never become conscious, and this comforting insight comes out of subtle reasoning that is part of Vedic *ātma-vidyā*. The *Rig Veda* has other insights that have potential in helping modern science resolve its crises in fields ranging from cosmology to medical science.

The Vedic idea of reality is one where materiality and consciousness are complementary aspects, like two sides of a coin, as in the standard interpretation of quantum mechanics, which is the deepest theory of physics without which chemistry and biology cannot be explained. Erwin Schrödinger, the Austrian creator of quantum theory, claimed in his autobiography that he was inspired to the central intuition of the subject by the Veda.

Sri Aurobindo, the great modern rishi, revitalized Vedic studies in the 20th century by his insightful commentary on key hymns of the *Rig Veda*. His books *The Secret of the Veda* and *Hymns to the Mystic Fire* revealed spiritual and psychological truths that had been forgotten for centuries. His interpretation aligned with his vision of spiritual evolution and the transformation of human consciousness.

Sri Aurobindo saw the Vedas as a profound source of wisdom and spiritual knowledge that could help individuals along the path of self-realization and freedom. He believed that Vedic seers had direct spiritual experiences which could be applied to contemporary times. His philosophy, known as Integral Yoga, aimed at integrating spiritual knowledge and practice with everyday life.

Yāska, nearly 3000 years ago, argued that Vedic mantras have three different layers of meaning: *ādhibhautika*, *ādhidaivika*, and *ādhyātmika*, which refer to physical, cognitive, and spiritual domains, respectively. This is reiterated in the Bhagavad Gita, where in 8.3-4, Krishna says that the *adhyātma* is the inherent nature of the individual, the *adhibhūta* is the perishable existence, the *ādhidaivata* is the inner self, and the *adhiyajña* is the divinity that is invoked at the ritual or the sacrifice. Sri Aurobindo uses these as the four ways of looking at the Veda: the physical, the metaphysical, the spiritual, and the symbolic. His decoding of the symbolic language of the Veda about the deities in the hymns opens up new spaces of understanding.

Notice that the term *adhyātma,* which is normally translated as the spiritual, is defined as inherent nature as each person's true nature is divine. Therefore, the way to obtain self-knowledge is to find one's own space of repose, which is in the light of consciousness. In the Yoga Sutras, Patañjali speaks of the awakened person as:

tadā draṣṭuḥ svarūpe'vasthānam || 1.3 ||
Then the seer abides in itself.

This knowledge is accessible to everyone as long as there is effort to leave those corners of our heart where the light is obstructed by the habits of the mind. This effort can be painful in the beginning for it involves leaving what the Bhagavad Gita calls *preyas*, pleasant, for what is *śreyas*, or good. It also requires moving beyond the mind, which is illuminated by the light of consciousness, to the light itself.

The knowledge of the Veda is called *trayī-vidyā*, that is triple knowledge. The triplicity may be seen in the division of the outer universe into earth, atmosphere, and the sun, with the corresponding divinities of Agni, Indra, and Surya, together with potential of transformation in Soma. Correspondingly, the inner universe is viewed as the body, the breaths or *prana*, and the inner lamp of consciousness. This triplicity spans reality as it is (*sat*), consciousness (*cit*), and transformation (*ananda*) that in the *saguṇa* form are represented by Vishnu, Shiva, and the Goddess.

The inner and the outer conceptions are mirrors to each other, and it is because of this mirroring that we are able to make sense of reality.

I am very pleased that Dr Pariksith Singh has written this book to demystify the *Rig Veda* for the modern reader by following on the path set out by Sri Aurobindo. He is eminently qualified to do so for he has studied Sri Aurobindo deeply and authored two other books on Sri Aurobindo's exegesis of the Veda, and he is a poet too; let us not forget that the seers of the hymns were poets.

Subhash Kak
Indian American computer scientist and
historical revisionist

Preface

The Veda is an ocean.

Of the purest and most condensed knowledge. And this ocean of wisdom is the heritage of all humankind.

This is perhaps the best way I can describe this ancient revelation of sacred hymns. Vast, multi-faceted, multi-horizoned, protean, revealing dimensions upon dimensions within its all-encompassing expanse. Each moment its colors changing, from aquamarine to chartreuse, from sapphire to violet, from indigo to emerald, from russet dawns to golden dusks.

And each colour a broadband of knowing, cognizing, experiencing.

It is an entire pageant of vibgyor—fluid reds, oranges, golds, greens, blues, indigos, and violets on display. Morphing into the shallows and gulfs at one place to the confines and bays at another, from the deep dark unknown in its nether depths to the wide sunny horizonless solitude of the open seas.

And the Veda itself mentions various levels or kinds of oceans. The *salilam apraketam* (*Rig Veda* X.129.3) is the ocean of inconscience that is beneath us, created by an involution of the Supreme Consciousness and out of which the Universe is evolving. The *maho arnah* is the great ocean above us (*Rig Veda* I.3.12), full of supramental light and knowledge that we can all ascend to. The term 'samudra', which means the gathering of waters, occurs frequently in the Veda and can also imply the vast all-embracing, all-pervasive nature of Varuna or Vishnu. The ocean as a body of water signifies the vast being of *Paramatman* or the Divine in Vedic symbology, the rivers as individual movements of consciousness or *chitta* in various capacities.

But much of this has not been understood. There have
been times these ancient hymns have been dismissed as
mere babblings of humanity in its infancy by early Western
commentators such as Monier Monier-Williams, Max Mueller,
and Ralph T.H. Griffith; or as *karmakanda*, or ritualism, by
the *Mimansaks*, culminating in the great Sayana; or confined
in the straitjackets of mere history and mythology as proof of
the Aryan Invasion Theory, invoking fanciful images of hordes
of horse-borne warriors rampaging across the plains of the
Indian subcontinent. Leopold Von Schroeder even compared
the Vedic rishis to his psychiatric patients. But the Veda has
a way of swelling and spilling beyond the confines of any
human barrier erected either by biases or intellectual theories
or any misreading. It rises, again and again, to flood all human
inhabitations by its unlimited and barrier-breaking vision and
reach.

All the various *panthas* or paths, philosophies, religions,
and cultures are but diverse streams flowing into its earliest
divinations.

If this premise sounds hyperbolic, let us examine it throughout
this book with an open mind. For we may find influences and
impressions from that age that we still carry in our subconscious
and which reflect in the confabulations of our daily lives. Perhaps
because it sings of what Carl Gustav Jung called universal
archetypes, bringing out the deepest secrets of human existence
with an intuitive and symbolic power.

After more than three decades of study and research into the
various aspects of Vedic mysticism, all I can do today is humbly
acknowledge that I have barely walked the sands of its shores
and waded through some of its beaches. Perhaps picked up a few
sundry shells lying in the surf or taken the occasional snapshot
of a moment. Every time I attempt to plumb its secrets and

explore its expanse there is persistent wonder at how much more remains unexplored.

What kind of singers were these rishis who refined poetry and enunciation to such a rarefied summit, all the while sharing the same images and tropes in the Veda? For anyone who has written *chhandic* or metrical poetry can aver how difficult it is to create one even with an original and individual inspiration. But to create hymns of everlasting beauty and power, using shared symbols in precise meters, exhibiting complete mastery of the material, emblazoning some of the best prosody and melopoeia in the history of mankind, is no laughing matter.

Indeed, while skimming through the Veda's rollers, the gentle laughter of its composers was still audible. The rishis were not a bunch of puffed-up and somber killjoys who claimed to have created it at all. Instead, they 'heard', and they 'saw' 'the waves of sound and light' as the mantras filtered through their consciousness without words in the limitless and ultimate sky of mind—the *parama vyoma*. And they chanted these *riks* or songs of light with utmost humility, gentleness, empathy, and in a spirit of liberation.

The Veda has been called *apaurusheya*, i.e., not created by man. It is true that all great art springs from a source that is no longer personal or individual. But their art was not only conscious in the highest possible sense of the word, but it was also collective, and it was also the defining literature for all humanity to come. Whether humanity realizes it today or not is another matter.

It is perhaps a testimony to this great achievement that their ability to create a collective or communal literature of such high culture has not been matched by any civilization to this date—at least as far as I know. And there are times when all I can do is marvel at the linguistic dexterity, complex symbology, virtuoso prosody, supple and extensive vocabulary, semiology and morphology, richly variegated sound-resonances, and foundational universal grammar that the rishis helped birth in this massive archive of compositions.

It is perhaps a testimony to their great achievement too that we have still not been able to adequately translate the Veda, numerous attempts at such an enterprise notwithstanding. The proud, and sometimes arrogant, translations by H.H. Wilson, Max Mueller, and R.T.H. Griffith stand discredited today even among Western researchers like Wendy Doniger and Stephanie W. Jamison since their interpretations of several key Vedic terms are not accurate (we have attempted to clarify some of these terms in the appendix). The theories about the origins of the Veda are yet to crack the mystery of its creation, timeline, or even the place of its origin; we can only guess, but we are never really sure. It makes us humble, this Veda. And it does not easily bend down to our dictates nor stay within our manmade reefs and shores. If there is one monument of antiquity that has much to teach us even today while it retains its mystery, it is the Veda.

Why is it important? To me, it is one of the highest watermarks of culture, art, and literature in human history. More significant a monument than even the Pyramids of Giza or the Great Wall of China. Even more importantly, it is one of the earliest documents of mankind's spirituality. And no mean document either. For it holds within its depths countless treasures and inexhaustible wealth that mankind has barely remembered to gather or value—resources that mankind may need again for its salvation.

It may be a blessing too that we have not soiled this most pristine collective heritage of ours. Do these nebulous beginnings of the discovery of its great wealth in our age portend a new stage in mankind's journey towards its own highest fulfillment and potential? Let us hope so. Dropping our biases, agendas, and presumptions, may we approach them as students and scientists, with a clean slate like the true inheritors we are to its legacy? This is a question that we need to answer with urgency.

For discovering the wisdom and the true cosmopolitanism of Veda may be key to mankind's very survival.

In our own times, to appreciate the Veda truly we needed a personality as wide, vast, noble, pure, and grand as the ancient rishis. Someone who could touch the heart of their poetry and the summits of their thought. Someone who was a seer and a visionary too, who could match their insights and their breakthrough discoveries, and who could understand and see what they perceived as an equal, knowing, in their own right, how they felt and sang. Such a modern master was Sri Aurobindo, the seer, poet, *darshanik* and *manishi*, yogi, and one of the greatest intellects of the modern age, who made the Veda available again to our generation. He unlocked the gateway, in the belief of many and this author, to a new Vedic age, which the ancient ones had foretold in their own manner.

In my opinion, Sri Aurobindo is the only one who has rendered the Veda into a foreign language with a vision equal to the original, elucidated it so that we can catch the inspired notes of the esoteric and mystical hymns. And then recreated new literary outpourings adapting the ancient Vedic symbols and the difficult art of the mantra to English verse. By understanding Sri Aurobindo, we can gain an insight into the Veda. Similarly, by appreciating the Vedic worldview we can better behold the beauty and compass of Sri Aurobindo as a poet and philosopher.

This book is an attempt to understand what the Veda is and how Sri Aurobindo brought it back to us in a manner analogous to the rishis—in a modern language and with modern tools but in a simple, lucid manner befitting a sage, genius, guru, and luminary of literature. Also, how his own vision shaped his reading of the Veda, and how his deeper, wider view of things gave him a new perspective on the Veda. We can study the correspondence and parallels between the two: Veda and the Integral Yoga that Sri Aurobindo emphasized. How the key to the Veda he elaborated helps transform our understanding of the Veda into a consistent progressive revelation of the ultimate challenges, possibilities, and means and ends of human existence. If only we can read the inherent mysticism and esoteric language and symbolism used by the rishis as a veil. It is this key that Sri Aurobindo provides us.

Because the rishis felt a profound affinity with the cosmos, its forces, and its constant changes, this intimate communion with the Universe is the reason for their style and composition. But without understanding this spiritual cosmogonic connection with the Universe, we cannot appreciate the Veda either. As the Veda points out, "Only the Seer can understand another seer, *kavaye kavyani nivachana*" (*Rig Veda* IV.3.6). Sri Aurobindo is that seer who has brought out its inmost secrets, more than anyone else in modern times.

The rishis saw life and their own existence as symbols of a deeper reality. But the symbol was not just fancy. To them, the "Symbol" expressed the "Real" intimately and experientially, and the "Real" was manifest in the live instant "Symbol". Or if one were to paraphrase him, "To them, the Real was the Symbol and the Symbol was the Real."

Sri Aurobindo has discussed this 'symbolic' stage of human existence with penetrating insight in *The Human Cycle*. The rishis saw life as a multi-dimensional play of forces and powers in a fundamental unity, which is reflected constantly in the Vedic compositions. To them, *yajna* or self-offering to the Divine was the key to the growth of individual and collective spirit leading it to *amritam*, or immortality, truth, harmony and universal good, or *bhadram*.

The Veda has now been made universally available by Sri Aurobindo as its original intent was. There can be no restrictions of caste or culture, religion, or nationality for anyone who wishes to study it. However, a deep immersion and preparedness is required to begin to understand the nuances of the Veda. Not just scholarly study alone, but a descent and surrender into its innate spirit, that was invoked and lived by its rishis. To truly appreciate the Veda, one needs to experience it, practice its unitary living, and open one's heart and mind to its vast Universe. For the Veda is primarily a spiritual document of highly advanced practitioners who expressed it in a unique manner. But it was meant for an esoteric reading, and this is openly stated in the Veda. It is *guhya* or hidden and deep. Understanding it profoundly changes our life, and without changing our life it is difficult to appreciate it in spirit too. Thus, this primer is an offering, an introduction, perhaps even a challenge to the perceptive mind that is comfortable with stretching its horizons and even (in this startup world) willing to disrupt itself.

In writing this primer, I researched Indic commentators such as Sayana, Swami Dayananda, Shripad Damodar Satvalekar, T.V. Kapali Shastri, Sri Anirvan, Amal Kiran, M.P. Pandit, Kireet Joshi, R.L. Kashyap, David Frawley, and Subhash Kak, among others. I also extensively surveyed the landscape of Western translators and analysts starting from Adalbert Kuhn, H.H. Wilson, H. Grassman, Max Mueller, R.T.H. Griffith, and Charles Sanders Peirce to more modern ones such as Louis Renou, Paul Thieme, Jan Gonda, Tatyana Elizarenkova, Calvert Watkins, Wendy Doniger, Stephanie W. Jamison, and Joel P. Brereton.

We are noticing a sea change in the attitude of Western commentators over the last 150 years or so. From the sometimes-less-informed stance seen among the earlier translators, such as H.H. Wilson, Max Mueller, and R.T.H. Griffith, who relied on the exegesis of Sayana and their own colored perceptions, Western theories, and concepts imposed on the Veda to a respect for its complexity, depth, significance, refinement, and mysteries by researchers such as Elizarenkova, Jamison, and Brereton. Modern scholars such as Wendy Doniger and Tatyana Elizarenkova accept openly that there is much to the Veda that they do not understand, and that their translations might have missed nuances that are vital to understanding the Veda's multilayered cognitive impact.

We are nowhere close to being done analyzing the Veda. We have barely conversed with the crash and roar of its surface. It is heartening to see an openness now to the various possibilities of its hermeneutics, especially among Western linguists, translators, scholars, and researchers, in works such as *The Rigveda* by Wendy Doniger and *Language and Style of the Vedic Rsis* by Tatyana Elizarenkova. What is missing, I feel, is the Indic perspective of spirituality in its interpretation. This process was begun by Swami Dayananda and expanded and deepened significantly by Sri Aurobindo. In fact, Sri Aurobindo and the Mother, Pondicherry, described experiences that are perfectly in line with several Vedic myths and descriptions, and their attempt to create a new future for mankind reminds one of the Vedic ideals of self-surrender, individual and collective growth, and self-transformation. Without this immersion in the spirit and the ancient mind of the Veda from an Indic *darshana*, its sense and meanings may not be wholly understood. An intense absorption is valid and necessary in the critical appraisal of any great literature, but the Veda is also unique in that no other literature of its time exists. And it needs reflections from the Indian mind just as it once needed it from the Occident at the initiation of its research in modern times. The spiritual, the mystical, and the esoteric is the missing element that needs to be brought out into its modern analysis and exegesis and that was first initiated in a detailed manner by Sri Aurobindo in our times.

Much more research is needed, of course, from the spiritual viewpoint. When I say spiritual, I mean it in the sense of the Indic term *adhyatmik*, which means that which pertains to the *Atman* or the Self of each individual. For as India develops its academic institutions and its own self-belief, we may see a greater depth in the doctorates and research of our scholars.

Sri Aurobindo's and the Mother's experiences of the cellular consciousness and the consciousness involved and hidden deep in the unconscious and the inconscient are singular instances of Vedic realizations in an emerging zeitgeist expressed in a modern tongue. But they need to be explored further in our academic publications and popular literature. For what is this zeitgeist, or spirit of the age? It is perhaps an ecological systems-oriented non-denominational approach to explore and discover hidden truths in our traditions without prejudice or preference—to find something that we have missed in our obsession with the outer and the technological, the physical, and the superficial.

I feel that a profound study of the Veda will show us how humanity evolved from a shared legacy and how we still live that inheritance, whether we realize it or not. And that once we appreciate how the Veda still holds us together as our collective spirituality and aspiration, we will see that all our vaunted differences are only on the surface. Deep underneath is the same still blue of the ocean that unites us all.

For we as humanity share not only our genes, but also our ancestral memes.

And the Veda sings this hidden oneness openly and joyously in its songs of light. We need to hear and see them now with our own *dhi-* or inner gaze or our *ketah* or intuition. Perhaps, it might be useful as a demonstration to quote T.S. Eliot here. The lines illustrate the extensive Vedic symbolism that he himself borrowed repeatedly from these ancient hymns in the *Four Quartets,* though in his own characteristic modern idiom:

The river is within us, the sea is all about us…

The sea is the land's edge also, the granite
Into which it reaches, the beaches where it tosses
Its hints of earlier and other creation:

...The sea has many voices,
Many gods and many voices.
                              The salt is on the briar rose,
The fog is in the fir trees.
                                        The sea howl
And the sea yelp, are different voices
Often together heard:
... under the oppression of the silent fog...

Acknowledgements

I wish to acknowledge my immense debt to Sri Aurobindo and the Mother, Pondicherry, without whom this book would not exist.

The Vedic rishis are the founders of our civilization. Without them, the Indian civilization would never have arisen in the first place, let alone taken the shape and form that it did. Modern India, too, in a sense is a creation of rishis such as Sri Aurobindo, who went into the very depths of ancient wisdom in their attempts to forge a new nation. This book is a tribute to the rishis, both of yore and of recent times—the *poorvebhih* and the *nootanai*.

I am grateful to Partho Dada and Makarand Paranjape, whose critiques and psychic scalpels significantly helped sculpt this guide. I am beholden to my parents, who tirelessly helped locate any reference I needed on a whim; my brother Reepunjaya and his wife Punita, for indulging my random demands and fancies to procure an everlasting supply of books; and Anirudh Chakravarty, whose unstinting support made the thought of publishing such a book possible.

I thank my wife, Maria Scunziano, MD, whose passion to help is a constant reminder of how the ancient and wholesome Ayur-vedic impulse to heal is still alive in the best of us; our four children, or 'kidneys'; and the fifth kid in our house, our pup, Mochi-ssimo.

And to you all for picking up the flame that the Veda reveals to us repeatedly in its hymns as a reminder of who we secretly are and of our unlimited possibilities.

A Note on the Method and Structure of the Book

This book is an attempt to approach the vast complexity and scale of the *Rig Veda* in Sri Aurobindo's light simply by using the key to these ancient hymns that he passed on to us. It is not an academic exercise but an attempt to appreciate, understand, and pass on the learning in as clear and lucid a manner as possible. For the Veda was, and is, a sacred text—a text that is shrouded in light and mystery and is one of the most complex and organic works of literature I have ever known. It is for those who love the adventure and challenge of an enigma and a riddle and the playful esoterica of the ancient rishis who witnessed its birth. For we have barely begun to crack its codes and conundrums, so cryptic and intricate is its secret. This primer is an attempt to bring out the key given to us by Sri Aurobindo in helping decipher one of the earliest literatures of mankind and one of its greatest mysteries.

My primary purpose here is to introduce the younger generation to the beauty and depth of the *Rig Veda* and seek Sri Aurobindo's help in decoding it—perhaps, in the process, to invite the young and modern mind to be inspired to read the *Rig Veda* on its own. For it is my firm belief and realization that the Veda conceals within its verses some great elemental truths that mankind sorely needs today to reach the next level of its evolution on earth. These truths, to my mind, are a universal harmony and brotherhood, a beneficent goodwill towards all and the discovery and experience of the intimate unity between the Self and the Universe. If this book succeeds in widening the vision of even one person, it would have served its purpose.

It is for that one reader, *Tad Ekam*, that I write.

It is also my belief that among the great modern exegetes and interpreters of Veda, Sri Aurobindo occupies a central place. I have used his key and paradigm to help understand the Veda. But I have not restricted myself to his commentaries alone. I have also taken the help of other masters, including the Upanishadic rishis and teachers of *Vyakarana, Chhanda, Nirukta,* Yoga, Tantra, modern Jungian and Maslow-ian psychology, Indology, Vedic studies, quantum physics, semiology, morphology, prosody, and linguistics. I have referenced them whenever feasible and shared a reading list at the end of the book that I recommend for further clarification and exploration of the Veda for those who might be sufficiently piqued and inspired.

When I use the term Veda in this book, I only mean the *Rig Veda*. The other three Vedas, i.e., *Sama, Yajur,* and *Atharva*, need their own specialized study and practice, which is beyond the scope of this book. All interpretations of Veda in this book are from Sri Aurobindo, unless otherwise specified.

This book is divided into four sections. Each is a different perspective on the Veda although the theme of spirituality hidden behind these ancient hymns is brought out throughout with the help of various tools and modes of reasoning and modern developments in human thought, literature, and communication. Broadly, these sections are the four considerations of Veda undertaken in this book: the physical, the metaphysical, the spiritual, and the symbolic, with the central motif of *yajna*. They are each separate and yet are only different ways of looking at the same canon. Like the proverbial blind men attempting to describe an elephant, each in his own way, each appropriate in his setting, yet incomplete, and even incorrect in the wider framework.

The first section seeks to contextualize the Veda in its historical, geographical, cultural, and religious setting. Here the attempt is to show its universality, despite a unique and specific location and associations in space, ethnicity, language, and time. And to also understand the sacred mission of India as a bearer of the Vedic torch, which must now be extended to one and all.

The second section deals with the 'model of the Universe' that is inherent in the Veda. Understanding this model with the help of certain clues may help us put future developments of human institutions and explorations like religions, philosophy, and linguistics in perspective, and help us discern how this paradigm is understood in reference to the vast *darshana* of Sri Aurobindo.

The third section is an attempt to decipher Vedic Oneness, inter-connectedness and Unity of Perception and Thought, which is distinct from monism and monotheism as understood in the Western and Abrahamic contexts. The objective is to gain an understanding of its non-exclusionary approach to life and to study the spiritual and philosophic applications and inferences from the Veda in our lives.

As Sri Aurobindo said in *The Secret of the Veda*,

[F]rom the language of the hymns we are compelled to perceive in the gods not only different names, but also different forms, powers and personalities of the one Deva. The monotheism of the Veda includes in itself also the monistic, pantheistic and even polytheistic views of the cosmos and is by no means the trenchant and simple creed of modern Theism.

It is difficult to explain this Vedic view that may be called a non-differentiation in seeing and being in present theological and philosophical constructs and contexts, and we will try to peel off the encrustations over our understanding to appreciate its unique Indic approach.

The fourth section focuses on the symbology of the Veda and the devas that are key to reading the ancient mind of the

xxviii   A Note on the Method and Structure of the Book

rishis to whom it was revealed. This section reads into the occult semiology of the Veda to gain an insight into its sounds, signs, codes, and formulae of speech, making them lucid and coherent. It attempts to explore the central motif of the *yajna* and how the four godheads of Veda—Agni, Indra, Surya, and Soma— facilitate its invocation, ascent, and success. The interactions of these four godheads or key devas in various dimensions is critical in the coming together of the Human and the Divine, one of the salient characteristics of the Vedic model of the Universe.

It is difficult to summarize the complex and multi-layered compilation of the Veda in one primer. My attempt has been to bring out a few intriguing and challenging aspects of these 'hymns of light' and elaborate on them by using the spiritual key suggested by Sri Aurobindo and my personal experience and intuition. This primer was created to prod, provoke, stimulate, encourage, and share, not to give categorical or definitive assertions for all time to come.

The reader might also notice some shifts in the narrative at times, especially while reading the translations of the hymns. I have attempted not to impose an artificial and smoother transition on the text of the Veda for its mantras leap from thought to thought, feeling to feeling, layer to layer, connected more by intuition than an artificial or mental schema. It is perhaps better for the innate connections and interpolations of the Veda to become apparent on their own to the reader at a deeper visceral level.

The *Sruti* has been compared to modern literature with its overleaps and quantum jumps by Stephanie W. Jamison and Joel P. Brereton in *The Rigveda*. I have tried to adhere to its sequence and collage-like interpolations, sub-texts and super-texts, echoes and recurrences, while holding on to its central threads or *sutras*. There is a logical interrelationship to the entire *Samhita* of Veda, whether we consider its symbols, or linguistics, rhythms or experiences, meanings or myths. But this logic is not a mental one. Its inherent unity is eventually to be found in one's own subliminal awareness that unveils progressively as one meditates on various aspects of the *Sruti*.

The other important element in the Veda is its recurring iterations of themes and symbols, each time with a different nuance, like musical notes in a grand symphony. I believe this makes it even more challenging since the shades of meaning may be more significant to those who use its text as a means of personal development. They are not so much repetitions as reiterations, aids in memory, to see various aspects of psychological movements as described by different rishis. To me, they are never boring or tedious but a reminder of the profusion of creativity from that period and in this text and the incredible subtlety of perception in each fine variation.

Any reiterations of the same concept, symbol, or motif, thus, are only to reinforce and re-suggest guidances that have been ignored by most commentators until now. Similarly, I have highlighted a few lines throughout the book that I believe are critical to understand in an exploration of the Veda. This is not only to emphasize certain key elements of Vedic study but also to align myself with what I call the tweet treats, in the fast-food culture of today's social (or anti-social!) media. In addition, one recurrent aspect of its method is to cite, throughout the text, a few hymns translated by Sri Aurobindo himself. These esoteric verses, with the Vedic keys to their symbolism interspersed throughout this primer, are meant to give the reader a taste of the original in the hands of the master translator.

I must clarify at the outset that this book is by no means an exhaustive analysis, and what is left unsaid might occupy libraries in itself. Yet, all simplification is but an initiative to reach the essence. In the attempt it misses out on much that is of singular beauty with its own integral relevance. I confess I have done so in a manner that does not do justice to the intricate *ragas* of the Veda. But since my attempt was not only to simplify but also to intrigue and fascinate the reader, perhaps the loose ends need to remain untied as an invitation for the readers to explore the text by themselves.

To me, the most important reason to attempt this guide and primer is that most commentators and translators of Veda have missed out its innermost significance and truth. That is so because they have not taken Sri Aurobindo's masterly interpretations seriously or have not approached with the intent of true scholars or researchers exploring the traditional and valid *adhyatmik* or spiritual interpretation of the Veda. This book is an attempt to redress this gap, as also to explain the key ideas in Sri Aurobindo's two masterly works *The Secret of the Veda* and *Hymns to the Mystic Fire*, written over a hundred years ago, which the lay reader may sometimes find difficult or abstruse without sufficient preparation. This note, I hope, will be one such grounding and initiation for a deeper plunge into the seven oceans of the Veda, which are all inter-connected and One.

I

The Veda: A Brief History and Context

1

The Six W's of the Veda

In the previous chapter, we have considered very briefly the special but vast and complex nature of our attempt to appreciate the Veda. In my opinion, this can be made easier if we approach its large corpus in an elemental manner. That is, consider the few but basic facts we know about it or can deduce in a reasonable manner. Armed with this information that comes to us from traditional and modern resources, we can perhaps begin to parse the more obscure and misunderstood aspects of its code and mystery.

When?

The Veda is one of the oldest scriptures known to mankind. We do not really know how old it is. Stephanie W. Jamison and Joel P. Brereton in their encyclopedic translation of its hymns *The Rigveda: The Earliest Religious Poetry of India* have estimated that it was composed around 1400-1000 BCE. However, this estimate is contested by other historians and commentators. Wendy Doniger in *The Hindus: An Alternative History* surmises that nomads in the Punjab region composed the *Rig Veda* in 1700-1500 BCE.

B.B. Lal in *The Rigvedic People*, with the help of archaeology, the radiocarbon method of dating, hydrology, and other allied sciences, has estimated that the Veda belongs to the 3rd millennium BCE. Georg Feuerstein, Subhash Kak, and David Frawley in *In Search of the Cradle of Civilization* use astronomical references in the Veda to determine that the *Rig Veda* is a creation of a period preceding 3100 BCE. Vedveer Arya in *The Chronology of India* believes that the Veda is at least 12,000 years old, based on his astrological and architectural investigations, although this has not been widely accepted in the scientific community. He is exceeded by Max Mueller though, who, in *The History of Ancient Sanskrit Literature*, exclaimed, "Whatever the age of the Veda may be, in one sense it is the oldest book in existence."

In my opinion, the Veda belongs to an ancient oral tradition that was extremely sophisticated and refined and predates the present estimate by at least a thousand years. Thus, we can perhaps surmise that it is about 4,000 to 6,000 years old. There are very few works of literature that are older than that. *The Epic of Gilgamesh* is considered to have been written as early as 1700 BCE according to Maureen Gallery Kovacs. Other ancient works such as *The Tale of the Shipwrecked Sailor*, an ancient Egyptian story, was written on papyrus sometime during 2000-1900 BCE. *The Book of the Dead* is a compilation of ancient Egyptian writing circa 1500 BCE.

But however we date it, it is unlikely that the enormous corpus of compositions that we call the Veda sprang up complete and autochthonous one fine day some thousands of years back. Rather, even common sense suggests that it was a part of a much older and evolving oral tradition and transmission, carefully preserved for hundreds of years prior to its canonical and standard forms. It is this feature that still makes it a "living" and evolving text, rather than a fossilized remainder from an all too distant and inaccessible past.

That is why we surmise that the Veda is not only one of the most ancient works of literature in human history, but the earliest organized work of spirituality and the most ancient, undamaged literature from antiquity that presents a coherent and comprehensive model of the Universe.

Why do I say "undamaged"? Because through all the upheavals and turmoil of Indian history, a most dedicated band of the keepers of the word transmitted it from generation to generation with an exactitude and perfection that staggers our credibility today. Through inter-generational memorization of millions of words, verses, stanzas, and compositions, they persevered, even at great costs and personal privation, what they believed to be the wisdom repository of the human species. Almost, one might think, in the same manner as our distant ancestors passed on the knowledge of how to build and maintain a fire so that the human race would not perish through the thousands of years of climate change or natural calamities. The Veda is, thus, a uniquely human heritage and gift. Why was it considered so valuable? What does it contain that is so essential to understanding who we are? It is our duty to come to terms with what it is trying to tell us.

The traditional Indic understanding is that the Veda is *Sanatana*, eternal and universal. Even when we say that its realization on earth or its 'composition' by the rishis who helped articulate the timeless happened at a particular moment in time. This intersection of the timeless and time is one of the wondrous explorations of Veda. And the Veda finds a fine balance between the eternal and the temporal throughout, without any sense of contradiction or paradox.

What?

The Veda is a *Samhita* or collection of verses revealed to or transcribed by rishis who were highly venerated in the Indian tradition. It is a selection of approximately 1000 *suktas,* literally 'well-saids,' which together contain nearly 10,000 *riks* or verses written in ancient Sanskrit or Vedic Sanskrit. Tradition has it that they were compiled by the legendary Ved Vyasa from the *riks* available in the lore at that time and he organized them in the present structure.

The oral tradition of the Veda, as noted in the section "When", is remarkable in that not only has its text been

preserved accurately since that time but also its precise
metrical intonations and pronunciations have been handed
down from generation to generation. This gives us a unique
opportunity to study a text that has remained unblemished
for nearly 4 millennia or more along with how it was articulated.
Compare this with what we know when we study the poetry of
Geoffrey Chaucer (1340s–1400 CE), and we do not even know
how it was pronounced when he wrote it and how he read it.
This availability of the Veda in near-pristine form is possible due
to the unique nature of the Indian tradition of how knowledge
is passed on by a teacher to his disciples, also known as the
guru-shishya parampara, and the immense prowess of the Indian
mind in its ability to memorize complex and interminable texts
forwards and backwards.

On the surface, these verses appear to be ritualistic hymns
that seek to propitiate forces of nature or a worship of devas
or 'gods.' These two interpretations are called *adhi bhautik*
(pertaining to the physical world) and *adhi daivik* (pertaining
to devas or beings of light). But there is a third interpretation
since the times the Veda was composed, and this is the
adhyatmik or spiritual tradition. This tradition holds that Veda
is primarily a record of spiritual experiences of the Vedic rishis
documented in a symbolic language that hides its true sense
from the uninitiated.

Where?

It is widely believed that the *Rig Veda* was recorded in the plains of
north and north-west India. To the Vedic rishis though, they were
'composed' not in a specific geography or locale but were seen-
heard in the *Parama Vyoma*, the Ultimate Sky. This understanding
itself perhaps may be taken as an illustration of their paradigm
of *lokas* or the multiple worlds. According to this paradigm we
inhabit multiple worlds (usually seven are noted in the Veda) at

the same time. Where action takes place, not only physically but also in spaces within that, are concealed from the usual eye.

Tatyana Elizarenkova in *Language and Style of the Vedic Rsis* calls Veda the first Indian text. The Veda has not just been preserved safely in its pristine form meticulously by the Indic civilization since its creation, it is dynamically alive, as we alluded to earlier, and several of its hymns such as the *Gayatri Mantra*, *Purusha Sukta* and *Agni Sukta* are part of the daily practice of Indic culture to this day. Vedic customs are still practised across the subcontinent during marriage ceremonies, *naamkarana* or naming ceremonies, *griha-pravesh* or entering home the first time, or cremation.

We can say this about the relationship between the Veda and the Indic civilization and India—the Indic civilization and India have been admirable bearers not only of the Vedic tradition but also its text and all the various *panthas* or paths that sprang from it.

Yet, despite being affiliated and identified with the Indic culture, as I have noted earlier, the Veda is a cosmopolitan and universal document that relates to all humanity. If it is considered only Indian and 'Hindu', then its global significance will be missed. Modern analysts such as Elizarenkova, Doniger, Jamison, and Brereton over the last century have begun to accept its wider influence and greater role in shaping the modern world, but we need to go deeper to enhance and augment our understanding and insights into our shared past and equally shared and more relevant present and future.

Who?

The Veda was 'composed' or seen-heard by the rishis as noted above. They were men of extraordinary calibre and wisdom, who were *kavis* or seer-poets, and masters of esoteric mysticism and its practices. Such men or women are described in various

cultures from that time, what is called the Age of Mysteries by Sri
Aurobindo. The various traditions that were part of this esoteric
mysticism belonged to the Orphic and Eleusinian traditions, the
priests of Egypt, the Magi of Persia and Chaldea, and the rishis
from India.

Who is a rishi? According to the *Rig Veda Samhitaa* by
P.C. Gautam, "The great Saayana gives the definition of Rishi
as *yasya vakyam sa rishih*, i.e., he who speaks (the words of the
Mantras) is the Rishi. The other accepted definition is *rishayo
mantradrishtaarah*, he who visualizes the Mantra is Rishi."

As far as we know, the rishis were not only mystics but also
occultists with a profound knowledge of the hidden workings
of the world. They were great poets and masters of various
sciences, such as Ayurveda, astrology, mathematics, architecture,
linguistics, prosody, musicology, and metaphysics. Some of them,
such as Vasishtha and Vishvamitra, are still revered in the Indic
traditions as mighty figures of great stature. Tommaso Iorco
in *From Veda to Kalki* says that they were as accomplished and
honored as later luminaries such as Sri Krishna or the Buddha.

The Vedic tradition reveres these ancestors who passed on
the torch of a different way of being to us. They are variously
called *pitras*, or *purvebhi rishi*, or with other epithets such as
angirasa or *ribhus*.

Why?

Why was the Veda written? We may conjecture that these songs
of light arose spontaneously as the rishis explored the truth of
existence. During their journey towards the truth, they recorded
these milestones and descriptions along the way. They found
that the discovery of the truth or *sat*, as they called it, also
brought about bliss or *ananda* and filled their consciousness
with an energy and a force that they called *chitta shakti*. This
sat is eternal and undying, *amritam*. Discovering this *amritam*

makes us immortal too. That is why the Veda is called the first gospel of immortality, truth, light, and bliss by Sri Aurobindo.

Why should we study the Veda? Is it still relevant today? Joel P. Brereton and Stephanie W. Jamison in their book *The Rigveda: A Guide* call it "a monumental text with signal significance for both world religion and world literature." In my view, this estimate is correct, and it will be accepted more and more widely with the passage of time.

The Veda is not only the oldest spiritual tradition of India that is available to us, but it is also the seed from which several future traditions emerged, such as Vedanta, Sankhya, Yoga, Tantra, and Bhakti. Even the so-called *Nastika* tradition of Buddhism has been influenced by it (more of this later in the chapter "Veda and the History of Oneness and *Sarvata*").

The Veda has also profoundly influenced Western thought, especially the pre-Socratic. For instance, Thales insisted that the Universe arose from water (reminding us of the *Salilam Apraketam* of the Vedic Creation Hymns); Parmenides stated that all existence is One (a la the *tad ekam*, That One, of the Veda); Plato saw the world of Idea that was hidden to our senses but is the truer version of the world we inhabit (this idea or 'Real-Idea' according to Sri Aurobindo is the world of *svara* or the sun-world of perfect form and existence); German metaphysicians like Hegel saw the world moving to a grand synthesis or unity; and Schopenhauer danced on the streets with joy when he first read of Vedanta for it expressed perfectly what he was trying to say in his philosophy. Moreover, some of the major wisdom-texts of religions like Judaism, Christianity, Islam, Buddhism, Confucianism, and Taoism seem to echo the notes of its grand harmony.

In my opinion, a working knowledge of the Veda and its key accomplishments widens our intellect and vision, and makes us truly catholic and all-embracing, something that our world needs desperately today. It is our shared heritage aspiring for the well-being of all mankind without discrimination or division.

And we need to bear its torch of universal benevolence too and pass its flame on to all and each.

How?

The Vedic rishis saw these mantras in heightened states of consciousness that they called the *Parama Vyoma*, the Ultimate Sky, as noted earlier in the discussion on "Where?" And all they did was record what they saw. That is why they are called *mantradrishtah*, or the seers of mantras. They became the facilitators or 'channels' in the transcription of these mantras in their inspired and refined states of awareness. They could give a sound body to these vibrations seen-heard in the stillness of the *Parama Vyoma* as they filtered through from the subtler realms to the gross, and this is their genius. Such vibrations in a perfect body of sound are called mantras, since they still have the capacity to make us realize the subtler and higher levels of our own existence hidden from us.

This is the reason that the Veda is called *apaurusheya* and also why it is traditionally called *Sruti* in the Indic tradition, which means that they were considered as revelations rather than creations of the imagination. (*Sruti* literally means that which is heard.)

In a sense, all great literature and art is impersonal, as T.S. Eliot famously emphasized in *The Sacred Wood*. And even our claims to personal authorship and glory of any work are shallow and markedly limited since we are hardly the sole doers of our actions—so conditioned are we in our thought processes and most of what we do. But the Vedic rishis turned creativity into a conscious process that was so refined that they could identify the source of their inspiration and took no credit for its origins. *Apaurusheya* then may not mean that the rishis played no part in arranging the hymns in a luminous manner or in facilitating their expression. Nor does it mean that they were entirely passive as in sessions of automatic writing. I see their consciousness as the ready and fertile soil in which the seed of the mantra fell and sprouted into gardens of bloom.

How do we appreciate the Veda? The study of the Veda is traditionally undertaken with the help of the six Vedangas, literally, the limbs of Veda. These are *siksa* (pronunciation), *vyakarana* (grammar), *chhanda* (prosody), *nirukta* (etymology), *jyotisha* (astrology), and *kalpa* (ritual). To these we may perhaps add the modern disciplines of linguistics, morphology, psychology, semantics, and the most ancient limb of Veda, *adhyatma* (spirituality), which is the practical application and lived experience of its *Sruti*. Let us try to figure out how the ancient and modern interpreters see its humongous body of text.

2

Interpreting the Veda

The Appraisal of Veda by Indic Luminaries

As discussed in the previous chapter, traditionally the Veda has been studied as a ritual, a myth or worship of devas, and as spiritual practice. Let us see how these three traditions have developed in parallel.

The ritualistic interpretation of the Veda was undertaken by the *Mimansaks*, prominent among them being *Jaimini*, *Shabaraswami*, and *Kumarila Bhatta*, according to T.V. Kapali Sastry in *Lights on the Veda*. Sayana who undertook an encyclopedic commentary on the Veda interpreted it too as a text of rituals. That is why they called the Veda the *Karmakanda*.

The earliest confirmation of the spiritual significance of the Veda comes to us from the Veda itself. It says clearly that the Veda contains mysterious and hidden words, *ninya vachamsi* (*Rig Veda* IV.3.16). It also states that the word only reveals itself to the wise or select, as a tender wife unveils herself to her husband, *uto tvasmai tanvaṃ vi sasre jāyeva patya uśatī suvāsāḥ* (X.71.4). *Taitariya Brahman* (3.12.9) and *Gopath Brahman* (1-33) highlight that without knowing the Veda, one may not know That which is great, and the Veda is like the Sun.

It is also clear that the Veda was held in the highest esteem by the Upanishads, which are traditionally called the *Gyanakanda* or the texts of knowledge. P.L. Parihar in his book *Vedas: An Insight* documents at least eight Upanishads along with their quotations honoring the Veda. This confirms that the Veda was held in high esteem by some of the most important *Srutis* in the Indic tradition, including *Kenopnishad, Kathopnishad, Brihadaranyaka Upanishad, Mundakopnishad, Taittriya Upanishad, Aitreya Upanishad,* and the *Shvetashvatara Upanishad.*

The Gita, also deemed a *Sruti* since it is considered the direct word of the Divine, *Narayana-Vak,* continued to honor the Veda in multiple shlokas, especially the spiritual interpretation of the first *Sruti.* Valmiki Ramayana, the *Bhagawat* and the Mahabharata again emphasize the great significance of Veda in the inner life of the spiritual seeker. *Sankhya Darshana* and Adi Sankaracharya similarly underscored the supreme value of Veda in the life of the society and the nation and for individual liberation.

T.V. Kapali Sastry in *Lights on the Veda* has shown that the tradition of interpreting the Veda continued through the next few millennia through the *Nighantu* of Yaska (around 500 BCE), Madhwacharya, and Raghavendra Swami. In modern times, Swami Dayananda and Sri Aurobindo wrote extensively about the spiritual meaning of the Veda.

Yaska

The great lexicographer, or compiler of the *nirukta,* Yaskacharya put together a dictionary of Vedic terminology at around 500 BCE. Of course, this date is also uncertain, given the lack of agreement on the date of the Veda. But what his etymological reference guide shows is that the Veda was already being interpreted for hundreds of years before our time. This continuous engagement with its meaning and significance is another index of how central it has been to our civilization.

Yaska's *nirukta* is thus the precursor of modern philology and semantics. It is a collection whose importance as a reference source has not diminished even after nearly three millennia. His work on etymology is critical also to understand the approach to linguistics or the *bhasha vigyana* of Veda. Indeed, he may be considered the founder of the science of etymology. Yaska preceded Panini, the master grammarian of ancient India. Panini wrote the *Ashtadhyayi* and mentioned Yaska by name, indicating clearly that Yaska was his honored predecessor.

It was Yaska who brought out the hidden *shlesha alankara* in the Veda, also known as the pun, and the fact that there are three layers of meaning in the Veda. Even by his time the meaning of nearly 400 words in the Veda was lost. That is why, without him it would be extremely difficult even to develop a basic understanding of the Veda, because Vedic Sanskrit is quite different from Classical Sanskrit in vocabulary, grammar, and sense.

Sayana

He is the great commentator from the 14th century who compiled the Veda and wrote an exegesis called the *Vedartha Prakasha*, literally, light on the meaning of Veda. Although he saw the Veda as a sacred ritual, he was also open to the possibility of a spiritual interpretation of the Veda. Early Western commentators and translators, such as H.H. Wilson and Max Muller, relied heavily on him as a source for their interpretation and gave their own non-spiritual rendering to the Veda. Modern scholars such as Swami Dayananda and Sri Aurobindo, in addition to later Western Indologists such as Jan Gonda and Wendy Doniger, consider his interpretations flawed and full of defects. However, for Sayana to have produced his monumental commentary in the most adverse of circumstances, when Muslim rule was in ascendance in India, is nothing short of miraculous.

Sayana is important as a grand compiler for preserving the original text and distributing it widely at a time when the Indic civilization was vulnerable to foreign invasions and rule. Thus, he may be used as a preliminary source. But he needs to be supplemented by Swami Dayananda and Sri Aurobindo to go deeper than the surface ritualism towards the hidden spirituality of Veda. For we must understand that, to our forefathers the act of the ritual was itself symbolic. As Sri Aurobindo perceptively points out in *The Human Cycle*:

> Take the hymn of the Rig Veda which is supposed to be a marriage hymn for the union of a human couple and was certainly used as such in the later Vedic ages. Yet the whole sense of the hymn turns about the successive marriages of Surya, daughter of the Sun, with different gods and the human marriage is quite a subordinate matter overshadowed and governed entirely by the divine and mystic figure and is spoken of in the terms of that figure.

Even now, the Vedic ceremony of marriage treats the whole *mandapa,* or wedding altar, as representative of the Universe. That sense of the symbolic and the ritual as a cosmogonic activity needs to be recognized and even the approach to ritual transformed. Mircea Eliade considered the Vedic ritual of *yajna* as an enactment of creation itself, and that is the correct insight into its symbolic significance.

Swami Dayananda

Swami Dayananda is one of the greatest scholars of Sanskrit that India has produced in the last couple of centuries. He was a social and cultural reformer, educationist, Vedic teacher, and one of the first Indian nationalists in modern times.

Swami Dayananda's most significant contribution to modern India was the bringing back of the Veda to the national consciousness, and it was the Veda of antiquity as originally perceived and created by the Vedic rishis in the spiritual light and not just as a rite of propitiation for gods of nature. He

showed with detailed analysis in his *Rigveda Bhasha Bhashya* that
Agni in the Veda is not just a flame but a *vachi* (which means
the articulator, expresser, or representative) of the *atman* and the
paramatman. The *yajna* of the Veda, likewise, is not just a ritual
but a profound action of spiritual invocation and self-offering to
the Divine, the *Ishvara*.

The Swami gave a clarion call to the nation to 'Return to the
Veda,' for in the Veda is our sacred knowledge, culture, truth,
and progress. By realizing its truths, he felt, we would recover the
glory of our land and return India to its dharma. He established
Arya Samaj, the society of the Arya, as one of the bedrocks of
Indian renaissance and social transformation especially in north
India. Rejecting the social evils of his time, including the caste
system and *Sati Pratha*, or the self-immolation of widows on
the funeral pyres of their husbands, emphasizing the education
and empowerment of women, he created for the Indian social
and cultural milieu the binding consciousness that helps hold it
together to this date. Even today priests from the Arya Samaj are
called to conduct civil ceremonies such as weddings or funeral
services in the Vedic tradition. The publication of educational
material and spiritual literature in national languages along with
setting up of schools and colleges across the country has been a
foundational activity for the dissemination of Vedic education
and acculturation.

How should we see Swami Dayananda today? While he was
a fervent votary of Vedic education, he rejected the Puranas
and later Hindu texts as inauthentic, full of distortions and
interpolations. He also trenchantly critiqued what he considered
irrationalities and inadequacies of other religions and darshanas,
like Christianity, Islam, Sikhism and several Bhakti traditions,
among others. This made Swami Dayananda controversial
and divisive and perhaps out of sync with the approach of
harmony that the new age needs. Yet Swami Dayananda is not
just a figure of historic, social, or cultural value; some of his

insights like asserting the monotheism of the Veda and seeing Agni as the *vachi* of *atman* and *paramatman* and his vision of human unity, among others, are still valid and deserve to be disseminated widely.

He was the first in modern times to create an awareness that Veda was indeed an important record of our history, civilization, culture, tradition, education, and spiritual past, and that it held profound truths that had been forgotten by us. And that if India were to realize its ancient glory, it had to rediscover its Vedic roots and re-live those truths.

He showed with detailed analysis in his *bhashya* that the Veda was not just ritualism of a primitive infantile race but the revelation of a highly evolved and refined culture that had much to contribute to India's eventual awakening. His use of *nirukta* or etymology in the analysis of the Veda brought back the Vedanga as one of the most critical tools to study the ancient hymns. He opened a line of further development in scholarship, cataloguing, and research into the *Sruti*, that may be of significance today as the Indic civilization is becoming more and more self-reliant and confident and is standing up for its own institutions and heritage.

He showed that all the devas or gods were manifestations of the same Reality. This Oneness or Unity, according to him, was the bedrock of the Veda and was the first articulation of that One Reality, *Tad Ekam*, in human history. Rejecting Sayana and his ritualism, he established the spiritual authority of the Veda once again in the Indian mind.

It is true that Swami Dayananda's message was given in a traditional language that the modern mind may need to simplify and decipher for future generations. But his contributions to the revival of Indian culture along the lines of Vedic traditions and learning are relevant even today. He was a warrior of light who burst on the scene when the entire Indic civilization was under the thrall of *tamas*, or dark inertia. And he gave it the mantra that the spirit of India may be awakening to, slowly but surely.

Sri Aurobindo

Sri Aurobindo was among the first commentators to apply modern critical methods of scholarship to the Veda. He used the concepts of linguistics as they had developed in his times and created a new field of what he called Embryonic Linguistics. He used etymology or *nirukta* to understand the devas and other key terms of Veda.

But Sri Aurobindo brought something else even more significant—the complete *adhyatmik* or spiritual interpretation of Veda, with clear elaboration of its symbols, *nirukta* and figures of speech in even greater detail than Yaska or Swami Dayananda, and a corroboration of its esoteric descriptions with his yogic experience, darshana, and worldview. Sri Aurobindo recognized Swami Dayananda Saraswati's unique contribution in reviving the Veda and then affirmed Veda as a record of some of the most remarkable spiritual experiences of the human species.

He ascertained and validated the traditional Indic understanding that indeed the Veda was a fountainhead of Indic mysticism and had much more that had not yet been fully discovered. He expressed in English what Swami Dayananda had begun in a national language, Hindi, and internationalized the insights of the great leader who had established Arya Samaj.

Sri Aurobindo showed us that the Veda was the seed from which grew the several Indic darshanas, religions, and Western philosophy. No other work of literature has ever had such an impact according to him. Sri Aurobindo saw in all the various religions a continuance of the original lights of the Veda, somewhat diminished or subdued, yes, but still radiant within certain exclusive or narrow frequencies.

One of the greatest intellectual achievements of last century is Sri Aurobindo's *The Secret of the Veda*. Its importance has not been fully realized even by Vedic scholars. His 'Foreword' to *Hymns to the Mystic Fire* is a giant leap for Indology and Vedic sciences, religion and philosophy, literature and linguistics, psychology and semiology, metaphysics, and spirituality.

3

India in the Vedic Light

We have reviewed the three traditional interpretations of the Veda in the previous chapter. It seems to me that these three interpretations define the way we humans approach life itself—from the gross perceptions to the subtler and psychological, and finally, the innermost or the spiritual. The unique feature of the Veda is that even the grossest interpretations of its meaning and ritual are imbued with symbolism and a mystic mysterious denotation.

That is why, to me, the Veda is non-denominational in every sense of the word. It bequeaths us a 360-degree view of life and allows each their own insight and perspective. Also, as the shared legacy of all humanity, it considers the welfare of the entire global human family equally in its hymns. And yet, the Veda is inextricably linked to India since the Indic culture has remembered its hymns faithfully and passed them to modern readership and audience in an almost pristine condition. How do we approach the Veda as the heritage of all humanity if it has been historically, geographically, linguistically, culturally, and spiritually associated, even identified, with India? And how does one justify then that the Veda belongs to all humanity? This is the question that the modern students of Veda and India may need to contend with.

For that we would need to understand how our ancient forefathers saw *Bharata* and its place in the comity of nations. Also, how India itself has inherited multiple dimensions of meaning from various analysts and scholars. At a cursory look, it may be deemed a landmass, a peninsula, and a nation of 1.4 billion people with its own constitution, system of government, electorate and place in the comity of nations. But it may also be seen as a culture and civilization that has carried the message, the symbols, and the motifs of the Veda in its society, institutions, and darshanas. To some, like me, India is a multi-dimensional vision, vast and integral, that encompasses a multitude of languages, ethnicities, cultures, belief systems, religions, philosophies, and even definitions of itself that contradict each other on a surface reading. This is important not only to understand Indian nationalism but also India's role in the future of the world and the evolution of humanity. Above all these descriptors just mentioned, India is also a Shakti, as Sri Aurobindo called it—a motherland of a thousand people and languages, cultures, and religions that teaches us immense tolerance towards its children in all their variances. And this is reflected in the names given to her by its adherents and dwellers, from the gross and physical to the subtle and spiritual.

Just like there are three interpretations of the Veda, there are (at least) three interpretations of India. India is a physical body with names of its gross body such as *Jambudveep*, India, and *Hindustan*. It is a subtler world of mythology and culture, as in *Nabhivarta*, *Aryavarta*, or *Sapta Sindhu*. Finally, it is a spiritual nation, a darshana as Raja Rao indicated in *The Meaning of India*, as *Brahmavarta* or *Bharata*.

India thus, can be seen as a purely physical entity, or a psychological-cultural agglomeration, or a transcendental-spiritual entity that affirms and fulfills itself. Each perspective has its own justification, etymology and development, and its own layer of interpretation. Each is also akin to the levels on Maslow's hierarchy of needs (which are the physical, the psychological, and the higher levels of self-fulfillment and, eventually, self-transcendence). Let us attempt to understand them one by one with an exploration of their roots.

From the *Sthool* to *Sookshma*, Gross to Subtle

Jambudveep is an entirely physical denotation of India as the
island or continent where *Jambu* trees grow. *Sapta Sindhu* or the
seven sacred rivers is another name often referred to in the *Rig
Veda*. John Keay in *India: A History* mentions that the Indus, to
which most of these seven rivers were tributary, was the *Sindhu*
par excellence, and in the language of ancient Persian, a near
relative of Sanskrit, the initial 's' of a Sanskrit word was invariably
rendered as an aspirate, 'h'. According to the Veda, these seven
rivers refer to the seven worlds or *lokas* (more of this later in the
chapter "The Vedic Model of the Universe"). Of these seven, the
river Sarasvati was considered the most important.

Some think nowadays that the Sarasvati was a mythological
river. And indeed, she is the name given to a form of the
Mahashakti, the one who is sweet, elaborate, focused on excellence
in the smallest details. She is the deity fit to be worshipped
or *aradhya* of the craftsman, the student, and the artist, who
works with the patience of centuries on the minutest and most
granular perfection, leaving nothing incomplete or unfinished.
The *Nadistuti* hymn in the *Rig Veda* (X.75) mentions Sarasvati
among Yamuna and Ganga in the west. R.L. Kashyap in *Rig
Veda Samhita* has compiled all the various references to Sarasvati
in the *Rig Veda* where she is given various qualities and titles,
including 'Flood of Inspiration,' 'Establisher of the words of
delight,' 'Possessor of Truth,' and 'Giver of Self-Expression.' It is
obvious that Sarasvati is not just a physical river in the Veda but
also a symbol of inspiration and, as Swami Dayananda noted in
his *Bhashya*, *divya vani*, divine voice.

Sri Aurobindo has proposed in *The Secret of the Veda*, "The
symbolism of the Veda betrays itself to the greatest clearness in
the figure of the goddess Sarasvati ... She is, plainly and clearly,
the goddess of the Word, the goddess of a divine inspiration." And
this, to my mind, is the best insight into the symbolic and spiritual

value of Sarasvati, no matter what her history and geography. Even if the Sarasvati has disappeared in body now, it lives on as a profound Devi in the Veda, an emanation and a force that has had a tremendous impact on the mind of India and her people.

Brahmavarta means the holy land or the land where the *Brahman* is known. *Aryavarta* in the ancient tongue meant the land of the *Aryas*—the term comes from the Sanskrit root *ari-*, which means to plough or to farm; it also means a person of self-refinement. Sri Aurobindo elaborates, "It refers to a cultured or noble person, which means that all (Rig Vedic) groups like to refer to themselves as *Aryan* ... The use of the word in a racial sense occurs in ancient Iran and modern Europe but not in India."

But beyond the levels of the physical, socio-cultural, mythical, metaphysical, and even psychological is the self-actualization of Bharata and eventually its self-transcendence in the sense that Maslow used these terms. Or to take the Vedantic paradigm, beyond the *sthool shareera* (gross body) is the *sookshma shareera* (the subtle body) of India. And further beyond is the *karanamaya shareera* (the causal body) of India's existence. The Vedic rishis looked beyond the surface and discovered a world of subtle influences, whether it was an individual, a society, or a nation. And they looked further still and found the core and the center that holds the subtle worlds and the surface appearances together. They called this center the *Karana*, or Cause. As we look at the hidden Cause or *Karana* of India or Bharata, it is a spiritual Consciousness and Force, a Shakti, that may be indefinable, yet eminently obvious and perceptible to anyone who is open and sensitive to it.

Indu, the Land of Bliss and Light

Aravindan Neelakandan in his extensively researched book *Hindutva: Origin, Evolution and Future* notes that the word Hindu does not arise from the mispronunciation of Sindhu by

the Persians as is commonly believed. But it is born of the word
Indu, which in the Veda meant Soma and the moon. Anirvan
in *Veda Mimamsa* notes, "Hiuan Tsang (had) given the name of
In-tou to the whole country; his Chinese ancestors used to call it
Chen-tou or *Tien-tchou* ... Herodotus (named it) *Indoi*. (And in)
Elamite (it was known as) *bi-in-du-is*." Arthur A. Macdonell
in *A History of Sanskrit Literature* voices the same opinion:
"Adopted in the form of *Indos*, the word gave rise to the Greek
appellation *India* as the country of the Indus. It was borrowed
by the ancient Persians as *Hindu*, which is used in the *Avesta* as
a name of the country itself."

We will leave it to the scholars and historians to figure out
the origins of the name Hindustan. Perhaps, at the end, it comes
down to how the next generation, in India and the world, sees
itself in the global fraternity and how it attempts to create an
awareness of the sacred mission at hand. Whichever source we
accept for the words Hindustan or India, whether *Sindhu* or
Indu, both arise from the Veda.

It seems to me that the ancient *pitras* or Vedic forefathers had
another understanding of India. They felt that the meaning of
the word Bharata comes from the root *Bha-*, which means light,
as in *Bhanu* or *Bhaskar*, which denote the Sun, and Bharata is the
land full of light. Thus, *Bharata* etymologically would comprise
Bha- and *rata* (*rata* meaning engaged or in search of), which
would mean that which is seeking for or is immersed in light.
The root sound *bhri-* also denotes light, and one of its meanings
is *dyoti*, which means shining or resplendent.

The root *Bhar-* also implies the bearer or sustainer, according
to Makarand Paranjape in his essay "India's Truths: Criticism
Across Borders for an Alter-Post Colonialism." This suggests that
Bharata would mean the bearer or upholder of light.

This might imply that there is an inner connection between
the names Bharata, radiance, light, seeking, discovery, and
upholding the Truth. Perhaps this is the idea of India that could

be its true definition, which we might want to consider. Why is this important? Because the Veda is "the first document of an original Indian culture" according to Tatyana Elizarenkova in her book *Language and Style of Vedic Rsis,* as we have discussed earlier. And the entire Veda is a solar hymn and a hymn of light—the light representing in its symbolism the highest consciousness of Truth and Being. Light thus defined is then the secret key, or at least one of them, to a definition of India, to an understanding of the Veda, and to the future of humanity.

The Veda has a pride of place in Sri Aurobindo's vision of a global awakening of humanity. He saw India as the bearer of the spiritual light and revelation it has carried on for ages, as the *Yuga Guru* and the *Vishva Guru,* the teacher of the age and the teacher of the world, respectively. But this can only happen if Bharata truly becomes once again the land upholding the torch of its ancient wisdom and carrying it through modern times. I mean this not in a parochial sense; India is a nation that is still most identified with the *Sruti* that most of us have forgotten, and it has a role to fulfill and a responsibility to bear this light with utmost sincerity and openness.

If this is the case, the entire understanding of India changes in the 'light' of Sanatana Dharma and Sri Aurobindo's vision of India's destiny and role in the future of humanity. The Sanatana Dharma was first articulated in the Veda as far as our available historic records go. Perhaps India and Hindustan then take their rightful birth from *Indu-* in the sacred hymns, the land of Soma, the drop of nectar, and the glow of the moon. This may also change our view of what the term Hindu means. The name *Bharata,* however, clearly denotes how the ancients saw this land, its people, and its mission on earth.

It was Sri Aurobindo who showed in his own life that one may be a fierce nationalist and leader of his civilization and people and yet be universal in vision and a lover of humanity. It is thus that I see the Veda. Within these contexts, as the ancients saw, the Veda is timeless and global, vast, and free of all contexts and limitations, collectively shared as our heritage and influence, and in its all-embracing aspiration for all mankind. At least the Vedic rishis did not limit themselves to a particular denomination except as warriors of light and children of immortality, *amritasya putrah*. Perhaps if we can recover their universal spirit, we too can find a truer unity and harmony in our world.

I close this chapter with a perceptive quote from Max Mueller in *A History of Ancient Sanskrit Literature* that illustrates my point succinctly:

> The Veda has a two-fold interest: it belongs to the history of the world and to the history of India. In the history of the world, the Veda fills a gap which no literary work in any other language could fill. It carries us back to times of which we have no records anywhere .... As long as man continues to take interest in the history of his race, and as long as we collect in libraries and museums the relics of former ages, the first place in that long row of books which contains the records of the Aaryan branch of mankind, will forever belong to the Rig Veda.

II

A Skeleton Key to the Veda

4

Twelve Sutras to the Veda

The Veda, as hinted earlier, is perhaps one of the most unique literary documents of our global heritage. To reiterate, it is essentially a sacred canon, one of the earliest stirrings of yoga and *adhyatma* or spirituality in humanity. If we miss its inner significance, then we miss its soul and its raison d'etre. For someone who meditates in and delves deep into his own consciousness and has even the slightest inkling of the subtler worlds, its secret is clear and unmistakable if Sri Aurobindo's key to the Veda is utilized. Only its symbolism needs a little getting used to. But it is my submission that the symbolism's unfamiliarity to the modern mind makes it even more beautiful, enigmatic, and profound—for it opens our psyche to something more elemental in ourselves, more archetypal, pristine, and resonant. If we can discover its key, the Veda transforms itself from an extremely complex and confusing text to the consistent comprehensive all-encompassing, all-embracing lyrical hymn of our forefathers, one that is highly relevant to our time.

What is this secret of the Veda? According to Sri Aurobindo in *Hymns to the Mystic Fire,* it is this:

> The thought around which all (Veda) is centred is the seeking after Truth, Light, Immortality. There is a Truth deeper and higher than the truth of outward existence, a Light greater and higher than the light of human understanding which comes by revelation and inspiration, an immortality towards which the soul has

to rise. We have to find our way to that, to get into touch with this Truth and Immortality, sapanta ritam amritam, to be born into the Truth, to grow in it, to ascend in spirit into the world of Truth and to live in it. To do so is to unite ourselves with the Godhead and to pass from mortality into immortality. This is the first and the central teaching of the Vedic mystics.

This truth, this light, is the core of our individual existence and that of the Universe. Finding it and living it is our purpose and secret fulfillment, whether we are conscious of it or not.

Sri Aurobindo adds,

> [T]here is a world or home of Truth, *sadanam ritasya,* the Truth, the Right, the Vast, *satyam ritam brihat,* where all is Truth-conscious, *ritacit.* There are many worlds between up to the triple heavens and their lights but this is the world of the highest Light—the world of the Sun of Truth, *svar,* or the Great Heaven. We have to find the path to this Great Heaven, the path of Truth, *ritasya panthah,* or as it is sometimes called the way of the gods. This is the second mystic doctrine. The third is that our life is a battle between the powers of Light and Truth, the Gods who are the Immortals and the powers of Darkness.

We have attempted to compile twelve *sutras* or clues to facilitate further exploration into these three central teachings of the Veda. We present them with a desire to promote further research and discourse among students and lay readers alike.

Sutra 1

The Veda is *adhyatma* in premise, essence, and experience. Yes, the language is ancient and arcane, but that is the living proof of its authenticity and antiquity. When we delve into it, it becomes obvious that the Veda is a text that hides layers and layers of meaning buried under a veil of symbolism and esoteric formulae of speech. To understand this spirituality, traditionally the principles of the six Vedangas may be studied, along with the keys provided by the Veda itself. But the secret to unlocking its esoteric and mystical meaning and validating it is *adhyatma* or spirituality, which is the true and ultimate Vedanga, as discussed in the section "How?" in the chapter "Six W's of Veda."

The Veda is a document of highly advanced spiritual realizations and is a *Sruti*, revelation. Modern commentators like Tatyana Elizarenkova insist that a study of later developments of Indian darshanas may not be used to retroactively fit their insights on the Veda. But it seems to me that studying the tree does indicate the nature of the seed that was planted. After all, if the result is a bloom of rose, we are not going to believe that seeds of poison ivy had been planted. We have every right to study the result, and from the nature of the result form a conjecture about the nature of the cause. Having said this, even such a 'diachronic' approach to understand the Veda is not mandatory in its study. The final validation of the Veda is in living and experiencing the *Sruti* directly and existentially.

Sutra 2

There are three layers of interpretation throughout the Veda. These are ritualistic, mythological, and spiritual. Yaska in his work, the *Nirukta*, says that all Veda contains three meanings: *trayortha sarva vedeshu*. These are the ritualistic, mythological, and spiritual. The spiritual interpretation is the most important of the three layers, as noted above, and without it the entire Veda becomes a husk of its true meaning and import. The Veda is a description of mankind's journey towards understanding itself in code language. And while it can be studied as poetry, history, anthropology, or a socio-cultural text, it will only make complete sense if we begin to understand the consciousness from which it was written and the mind that was its first witness.

Sutra 3

The language of the Veda is symbolic, hidden with *shlesha alankara* or puns, complex figures of speech, signs and codes, polysemy and synonymy, and many other literary devices that play with its vocabulary, morphology, semantics, and semiotics. Even numbers or variations of rhythm are symbolic and have a deep significance. Once these symbols are understood, the entire Veda becomes simple and clear. Through this symbolism, through 'language-painting', a term first used by Paul Thieme, and various figures of speech, the Vedic rishis deliberately created a system of parallel meanings, at least at three levels, as noted above.

Thus, terms like *gau* mean both cow and rays of light, *ashva* means horse and vital energy, *ghritam* is purified butter or luminous and a clear, dense state of mind. Similarly, Soma is not an intoxicating drink derived from some special herbs, but the bliss or *ananda* produced by yogic *askesis* or *tapasya* that transforms our life-energy or *prana*, mind, and body. (More on this in the section "*Yajna* and the Fourfold Godhead of the Veda.")

The primary means to unlocking this symbolism is *adhyatma* or spirituality. Others are *nirukta* or etymology, the mantras, linguistics and semiotics, other Vedangas, and a study of Veda from the keys provided by the Veda itself.

Sutra 4

Non-duality or unity is a dominant theme throughout the Veda, in each mandala, and is not a product of later developments. Each deva is a manifestation of the hidden unity of the cosmos, the One Reality, *Tad Ekam, Tad Satyam, Tad Adbhutam*. This sense of Oneness is clear throughout, and we will discuss this in detail later in the chapter "Veda and the History of Monotheism" in the third section of the book. This Wholeness or *Sarvata* is dominant throughout the Veda, but the wholeness of Veda is more dynamic and alive than the present conception of the word in the West.

Vedic non-duality is not flat and abstract like the Monism of Spinoza. Each manifestation of the One Reality or *Tad Ekam* can assume its fullest grandeur and powers without losing its fundamental unity and identity. Thus, Soma can be a deva and yet in some hymns be the all-powerful Surya itself and become the Divine. And yet, Soma never loses its particular and specific function and significance in the overall scheme of things. The Divine in the Veda is both form and formless, and yet is always beyond and escapes our human conception and restrictions of language.

The Vedic hymns reflect a profound identity felt with the entire universe by the rishis, such that there is no separation between the individual and the cosmos, and this mystical experience is the basis of all further darshanas and religions.

Sutra 5

Devas are not independent gods but powers and manifestations of the One Reality, One Truth. These devas are not gods as depicted in Greek mythology, but supra-physical forces of harmony that assist the seeker and yogi in their spiritual growth. They are not imaginary figures but *shakti* of the One Truth and can be independently experienced, verified, and validated. Each deva is a power and a symbol, a force that can be concretely experienced by one who develops the subtle insight or even an empathy to the concept.

Deva means to shine from the root *div-*. In all major religions, we have such beings that assist humanity in its seekings. In other religions they are given various names, such as angels (derived from Vedic *angirasa* according to David Frawley) or *farishtey* (etymological origin is the Sanskrit *presyata*, which means to send), among others. These shining ones are supra-physical beings, forces or realities that we can grow aware of and invoke to help us in our journey on earth.

Sutra 6

The battle between light and darkness, the devas and *dasyus*, is first described in the Veda and is a recurrent theme through all major religions even today. These *dasyus* are not Dravidians but forces of inertia, pride, and darkness that obstruct the growth of the *sadhaka* or the yogi. One may perhaps make a case here that the tremendous openness and dynamic unity of Veda and its original Sanatana Dharma gets narrowed and distorted in other religions, specially their exoteric expressions.

The word deva has multiple meanings in the Veda, depending on the context, according to P.C. Gautam in *The Rig Veda Samhitaa*:

> It may mean the Almighty Supreme God, the demigods of the legends, the polite address among friends and anything or being that is praised by a Rishi.... Learned commentators in the past have not been able to agree to a common definition (of a deva) ... *Ya rishinochyate sa devata* (The one praised by rishis in their mantras is a deva).

We can see that the devas defy easy or summary definitions and are symbols as well as real, abstracts as well as entities, who can impact our life and help us if we learn how to invoke their powers. Sri Aurobindo in *The Secret of the Veda* elucidated that the devas are "not simply poetical personifications of abstract ideas or of psychological and physical functions of Nature. To the Vedic seers they are living realities... not merely principles and tendencies but of the cosmic powers which support and embody them."

Sutra 7

The *yajna* is not 'sacrifice' as usually understood. For sacrifice implies a loss or self-abnegation in the modern usage. But *yajna* means self-offering and self-surrender to the Divine. It is the central concept of Veda and means, among other things, Vishnu, Shiva, Yoga, Dharma, offering, invocations, etc. *Yajna* is also not a ritual that is held to propitiate gods of nature and to gain riches, sons, armies, cattle, horses, and victory over enemies, land, and happiness. Neither is it human sacrifice or *narabali* (of which there is not one incident described in the Veda), nor those of animals. One of the roots of the *yajna* means to join. So, it is about joining the human and the divine within and without.

The use of the word 'sacrifice' as an equivalent of Sanskrit *yajna* was a grave error committed by H.H. Wilson, perhaps influenced by his Christian background and 'legends of the Old Testament,' according to P.C. Gautam. Monier Monier-Williams corrected him and translated *yajna* half a century later to mean "worship, devotion, prayer, praise, act of worship or devotion, offering, oblation…" (*Yajna* is discussed in more detail in section 4 of this book.) However, if we go to the etymology of the word sacrifice, we come to face the forgotten fact that it arises from two roots, *sacer* and *factum*, to make sacred. It is the subsequent imposition of loss over its original sense that detracts from the meaning of *yajna*. Either we need to recover the original meaning of the word sacrifice or replace it with other words more in line with the sense of the word *yajna*.

Sutra 8

The mantric vibrations and intonations of the Vedic *riks* create another level of experience of the hymns and, if one is open enough, unlock new levels of perceptions and resonance in the listeners. This approach to poetry is unique in world literature. It is true that there is a secret aspiration towards an inevitability of expression in almost all verse worth consideration. The seer-poets of Veda and other *Srutis* show a singular focus on the ability of their poetry to bringing out such symphonic and reverberating sounds and their echoes.

Mantra or the highest expression of sound, meaning, and vision is the greatest realization of the Veda. It confirms the tremendous refinement of culture at the time of the Veda. The mantra is a unity of thought and speech, sight, and sound. And the mantra can be read or recited, chanted, or sung, and there is a science behind its pronunciation too. For the resonances of sound create a new layer of meaning that takes off from the literal and the phonetic and becomes its own language.

The mastery of each note, sound, syllable, and their combinations is critical. For the seed sound, or *beej dhvani*, has its own experiential meaning. The use of harmonies and resonances are akin to that of a raga of these seed-sounds, and one must listen with deep and total attention and develop an appreciation of the possibilities of words and their combinations. Thus, the mantra communicates on various levels, the verbal and the non-verbal, the literal and the symbolic, the metric and para-metric. Perhaps it is only appropriate to note here that the highly treasured and appraised melodic framework of the Indian classical raga evolved from the sounds and principles of the Veda.

The mantra opens multiple dimensions of experience to the reciter and the listener. Expansions of perspective, a widening, a heightening, a deepening of consciousness, as with great art in which the beholder is transformed, is the sine qua non of its appreciation. But the mantra is complete only when it is chanted with devotion and concentration, repetitively, until it rises and falls with each breath, and becomes an integral part of the physical, mental, and emotional consciousness of the aspirant. The secret knowledge of using sound as a means to reach the Divine was first revealed in the Veda.

Unfortunately, we are unable to recreate the experience of Vedic mantra on these pages, since to accomplish that one must not only be able to read Vedic Sanskrit but also be able to intonate and enunciate it correctly. To those who may be interested, for such an experience we recommend recordings of Vedic chanting done by recognized schools, which are also available online.

Sutra 9

Veda then is a journey towards truth, harmony, immortality, and universal benevolence or *bhadram*. If one understands its key terms such as *Ritam*, which means Truth in manifestation, and applies it consistently throughout the text, the obscurity is removed, and the Veda becomes a homogeneous record of a man's inner search; the first successful attempt was made many ages ago.

This spiritual journey, *Adhvara*, is described in various forms in the Veda: as a journey across the waters of being, or *apas*; as an ascent along the hill of being, or *adri*; or as a battle of the forces of light (devas) with those of darkness (*dasyus*). Another term that is used is *svadha*, which implies the good or the benediction that comes from being true to one's nature, with authenticity or dwelling in one's own nature or *svabhava*.

The Veda affirms life in all its aspects. Not for it a rejection of mind, life, or matter, or escape from the world. Nor is there the schizophrenia of duality that some later theologies have been afflicted with. It accepts all aspects of life and aims to transform them. And Vedanta is not a revolt against the Veda but only a flowering of these ancient discoveries.

Sutra 10

The Veda's impact on modern life may be noticed if one begins to appreciate its foundational influence on almost all aspects of modern human life. It has been a powerful influence on all Indian darshanas, Greek and German philosophy, linguistics, literature, poetry, culture, and several religions of the modern world, including Judaism, Christianity, Islam, Confucianism, Buddhism, and Zoroastrianism. We can see its influence across the globe even today. The Veda may be seen as a residual influence on almost all aspects of our life to this date, and it may even be an important factor in our evolutionary future.

The battle between the forces of light and dark (as discussed in the section on devas) is a constant Vedic theme that is a permanent imprint on religion, art, and narratives even today. So is its depiction of the devas, which are seen in various forms in all major religions. European culture, psychology, and linguistics have been shaped by ancient Vedic discoveries.

Sutra 11

Even myths are symbols and descriptions of spiritual experiences. Indra destroying *Vritra* is not the battle of mythologic beings but the luminous mind within, breaking through the obstruction of ignorance and narrowness of energy in the higher mental faculties. *Vritra* is the obstruction of higher knowledge working in the lower parts of our being, i.e., body, *prana*, and mind. *Vritra* is destroyed by Indra, the luminous mind, by using his thunderbolt or power of lightning with the help of Sarasvati, who is the inspiration or revelation from higher states of truth and consciousness, and *Angirasa* rishis.

Similarly, *Vala* is the hiding of the rays of light or knowledge in the darkness of matter and unconsciousness. The myth of *Vala* is Indra recovering the hidden knowledge and rays of the sun in the inconscient or *Adri* with the help of *Sarama* or Intuition. The same symbolism is seen in the myths of the Creation hymns and legends, such as those of the *Angirasas* or the legend of *Shunashepa*.

Sutra 12

The Vedic Universe comprises seven *lokas* or worlds, ranging from the highest consciousness to the densest matter and unconsciousness, like a spectrum. The Veda sees the human as a multidimensional being who encompasses all these *lokas* in his or her own self. Thus, each human holds within himself or herself all the seven worlds including the highest ranges of truth, consciousness and bliss, and the One Reality, *Tad Ekam*. And it is the individual's highest calling or possibility to reach the highest ranges of existence, incorporate them in his being, and live a life of joy, success, victory, self-mastery along with mastery of the worlds.

This spectrum of *lokas* creates a paradigm of the Vedic experience that is consistent, coherent, and comprehensive. The diverse aspects of existence, even those that seem to be polar opposites, are accepted in its spread, each with its own validity and place in the universal scheme of things, and the widest discrepancies harmonized in its iridescence. The concept of *lokas* also helps in understanding modern theories, like synchronicity as offered by C.G. Jung where acausal connections between the physical world and the psychologic worlds are seen.

All these twelve keys or sutras are inter-related and interconnected in the true unity of the Universe, or *Tad Ekam*, The One, which can be experienced, lived, and expressed in thought, feeling, speech, and action.

There are more keys to understanding the Veda, but I feel these are sufficient for a basic understanding of our ancient heritage. More research and study may be undertaken as needed. As one peels off the superficial understandings, one may find that the Veda is a veritable onion, with layers within layers of meanings, dimensions, and experiences couched in its mystical formulae and codes. Rest is personal growth, immersion in its temporally distant but still relevant and applicable psychology and poetry, and letting its harmonies work through the consciousness. One hopes that this modest primer will stimulate further exploration along the lines suggested by Sri Aurobindo, T.V. Kapali Shastri, and Swami Dayananda, among others.

I also believe that if scholarly and academic research is undertaken along the spiritual import of the Veda, the contradiction between the reverence shown to the Veda as a *Sruti* in the Indian traditions and its relegation to *karmakanda* or ritualism may be resolved. For the Veda is quoted and referenced in the Upanishads, the Gita, and the later traditions such as Tantra, Vaishnava bhakti, *Dvaita* philosophy of Madhvacharya, and Swami Dayananda, among others. Once we understand that in the synthesis of Veda and Vedanta all these *panthas* or *margas* are contextualized in a larger framework and order, and the dichotomies are resolved in a paradigm that is not closed to variations or divergences.

5

The Vedic Model of the Universe

The Individual as Hologram

The Vedic 'model of the Universe' is not very complex. Its beauty
is an essential simplicity leading to infinite variety and complexity.
It fundamentally perceives the Universe as a perceivable verifiable
unity, which manifests itself in multiplicity. Innumerable names
and forms, modes of expression of its primordial energy are what
give the unity great diversity and variability. And yet this unity
is not in opposition with the diversity. The unity is glue to the
variety of the world. As Sri Aurobindo said in *The Life Divine*, it
is the One as Many and Many in One.

The Veda sees the Universe as a partnership of the human
and the divine, the individual and the cosmic, the self and the
other. There is barely or no demarcation between the inner and
the outer, the physical and the psychological.

In the Vedic paradigm, the Universe is a representation
of the individual, and the individual a representation of the
Universe. Tatyana Elizarenkova calls this 'isomorphism' in the
Language and Style of the Vedic Rsis. R. Narayanswami in his book
Understanding the Vedas terms it 'equivalence.' Sri Aurobindo
calls this 'correspondence.' Thus, the human is the hologram
of the cosmos. And this is not theory for the rishis but is real
actual, dynamic, and practical. By transforming oneself one may
impact the Universe and vice versa. Similarly, the powers in the
external world are inseparable from the powers of the mind and

vitality within. And the outer world is a symbol of the reality within. Thus, the lightning of Indra is the flash of enlightenment within one's mind. The Surya or Sun is the principle of the highest creative power of the world, the principle of Truth, Consciousness, and Bliss or *Sat-Chit-Ananda*. It is the highest supramental awareness possible to us. The earth is represented by the body, the sky is represented by the mind, and Agni is the fire burning within the heart that is the Divine within us.

The entire external world is but a projection or creation of the individual's consciousness. This reflects the profound oneness that our ancient forefathers felt with the Universe and that is why it was clear to them that the world outside cannot be influenced without changing the world within.

The individual is thus not only a part of the Universe, he or she is also the fullest symbol and 'fractal' of it. This insight later flowered in the mighty realizations of Vedanta and Tantra in Indian spirituality and yoga.

This in simple words is the Vedic conception of the place of the individual in the cosmos. Or shall we say, the Vedic conception of the unity and the mirrored equivalence of the microcosm of the individual and the macrocosm of the Universe. It is the same systemic and ecological connection between the human and the external world that some modern sciences are attempting to explore today. Only the rishis of the Veda reached this sense of oneness with all creation and all creatures, through intuition and an openness of heart and mind that even today is refreshing and rejuvenating.

But this state of unity is not abstract or theory. Ancient Indian traditions since the beginning of the Veda have placed great importance on personal corroboration of evidence or *pramaana* and verifying it oneself. This *pramaana* is not intellectual mathematical proof but the validation of direct perception and being. *Suchetasam anubhavah pramaanah tatra kevalam* is an ancient formula articulated in different ways, as elaborated by

Tommaso Iorco in *From Veda to Kalki*. It means that the direct experience of an awakened (enlightened) awareness is the only evidence. Thus, to the rishi it is an unfiltered knowing that is not dependent on the senses or external data or even personal perspective or emotional sensation. And that is why tremendous value has been placed in the Vedic Vedantic traditions on liberating the consciousness from its bondages, discursions, distractions, and movements, until it reaches a state of pure awareness that is instinct with knowledge and the self-proven and self-realized evidence. It is a higher level of existence than the *Homo agitans* (the disturbed man) or *Homo cogitans* (the thinking man), that most humans are, and is truly the mark of *Homo sapiens* (the wise man). And this perception of the *pramaana* is its own radical transformation of the seeker's awareness. That is, the experiencer becomes the experience, the rishi becomes the *pramaana*.

In other words, the rishis saw the world with a refined and evolved consciousness. And they experienced the world in a manner that the normal human being does not. And yet, their realizations were methodical, detailed, scientific, and precise and not idiosyncratic—as granular as a scientist in a laboratory. And their perceptions give us at least as consistent and coherent a view of the world as modern science with its yet nebulous probings. Their *pramaana* is lived, universally repeatable and profound, if one experiences a higher awareness by a process of personal development.

The Paths of Yoga and Yajna

This sense of unity with all creation and creatures achieved within one's own heart through personal evolution and direct realization is the secret of all mysticism and spirituality that developed in the Age of Mysteries. And from it sprang the disciplines of Yoga (the word Yoga means to add or join), the great insights of Vedanta that the *Atman* is the *Paramatman* and the puissant *marga* or path of Tantra (which sees all manifestation as the single principle of Shakti).

Let us look at the very first Sukta of the Veda called the *Agni Suktam*. The 7th *rik* of Sukta 1, Mandala 1, 3rd *pada* says,

नमो भरंत एमसि
We bow to you (with our *dhi-* or thought)

Or as Sri Aurobindo translates the whole mantra much more elegantly, "To thee, O Flame! We day by day, in the night and in the light, come, carrying by our thought the obeisance."

We can see that Bhakti or devotion and surrender come very early on in the Veda, although it gathered self-offering and seems to be quieter than later Bhakti movements. This is critical to understand. Even the word ईल, usually translated as praise, signifies love or adoration if we go to its etymology. This is how Sri Aurobindo translates the first mantra of Veda from the *Agni Suktam*:

अग्निमीळे पुरोहितं यज्ञस्य देवमृत्विजम् ।
होतारं रत्नधातमम्
I adore the Flame, the vicar, the divine *Ritwik* of the Sacrifice, the summoner who most founds the ecstasy."

R.L. Kashyap translates it thus, "Agni I adore, placed in front, the God of *yajna*, rtvik or one who has the ecstasy of Truth. He, the summoning priest, activates (in human beings) the dormant ecstasies excellently."

The meaning is clear if we understand the symbolism of Agni standing for the Divine in our hearts, the *Atman*, the Divine Love. Satprem in *Anti-Matter*, brings out the same point in his inimitable manner:

Nor was it insignificant that fire, Agni, was the core of the Vedic mysteries: Agni, the inner flame, the soul within us (for who can deny that the soul is fire?), the innate aspiration drawing man towards the heights; Agni, the ardent will within us that sees, always and forever, and remembers; Agni, "the priest of the sacrifice," the "divine worker," the "envoy between earth and heaven" (*Rig-veda* III.3.2) "he is there in the middle of his house." (I.70.2)

Let us also look at the 9th or last *rik* of the *Agni Suktam* as translated by Sri Aurobindo, "Therefore, be easy of access to us as a father unto his son, cling to us for our happy state."

A close intimacy is sought, as of father to son. In this light, the whole *Agni Suktam* becomes more than a ritual or praise, *stuti*. It is a description of the inner qualities of Agni, as felt profoundly by the rishi. It is an invocation of the Divine in us, the revelation within, and the surrender and self-offering to the Divine. Nor is it a distant relationship but one as close as a human bond can be. It is a realization of the powers of Agni and how it is the leader in the personal growth of the seeker. All this is stated symbolically but the sense is obvious if we peer beneath the surface of its veil.

R.L. Kashyap in the *Rig Veda Samhita* explains thus,

> This hymn (*Agni Suktam*) ... contains the seeds of the Bhakti tradition, particularly in the seventh and ninth verses. Agni is not a mere flame or even the deity of flame. He is a special aspect of the Divine whom the rishi loves with intensity comparable to the supreme Bhakti described in later devotional literature.

He also points out with insight how even Jnana Yoga appears in the first Sukta of Veda or the *Agni Suktam*. He says, "The seventh verse indicates that the Rishi-s were familiar with the techniques of meditation, i.e., directing the thoughts. The idea of surrender, developed later in the Bhakti literature, is already present here. Here we see the mingling of Knowledge and Bhakti."

R.L. Kashyap was profoundly influenced and impressed by Sri Aurobindo's exegesis and explanation of Veda, its symbolism, and latent meanings. And he has brilliantly elaborated on the later yoga that is already present in seed in the Veda, applying the tools of artificial intelligence to his research. The third aspect of Yoga, the Yoga of works, or Karma Yoga, comes from realizing that Veda is an integral approach to life.

For the Veda is an affirmation of life, joy at the creative play of the world, and wonder at the mystery of every object, movement, and person. There is not the emphasis on escape from life's challenges; rather, such an approach arises out of ignorance or misunderstanding. Nor is there any attempt to see the world as an illusion or falsehood.

The Veda does not reject matter or the body; nor does it run away from life. It does not look down upon the mind either. It embraces each aspect of our existence and attempts to transform them all in the higher vision, light, and bliss. For in matter too is the truth of the highest level of our existence. Thus, Karma is an important aspect of human life, and no aspect of life is shunned.

In Mandala 1, Sukta 2 of the *Rig Veda*, the first *rik* invokes Vayu, which represents *prana* or vitality to partake of Soma, the bliss. After this, Indra is invoked and invited too. This indicates that there was an awareness of mastering *prana*, perhaps an early insight into *Pranayama*. So, also, there was an awareness of mastering of oneself through self-purification, self-control, and mastery and concentration, *dharana*, leading through the various stages of Patanjali's Yoga that was to develop later.

The First Gospel of Immortality and Bliss

The essence of the Veda is the search for Truth, Light, Bliss, and Immortality. This is brought about by a transformation of all parts of oneself, including body, *prana,* and mind by opening oneself to the wideness, light, joy, and dynamisms of the higher levels of consciousness that are also an integral part of the being we call the human. In a practical way, the purification of Agni, the surrender of all of oneself to it, the intensity and the *Tapasya* or *askesis* of the *yajna*, create a psycho-physiological alchemy within. This alchemy by fire, this divinization, creates bliss, which is also called Soma, the sense of joy that comes out of pure being.

This Soma is highly prized as one of the secrets of the Veda. For this, bliss needs to be held and stored in the *kalasha* or vessel of the heart. And it is offered to *prana* or Vayu deva and Indra or the higher ranges of mind to act as a catalyst and agent for their metamorphosis. In Mandala 1, Sukta 2 of the *Rig Veda*, the rishi invokes Vayu, and Mitra-Varuna, and later *Vishvadeva* to come and partake the Soma. The significance would not be lost on serious practitioners of Yoga. For bliss transforms mind, body, and vitality, purifies the emotional mind into a wider gentler kinder nature, and this *kriya* of Agni or Action was very well known to the Vedic rishis and practiced by them. Until bliss rejuvenates and vivifies the practitioner and opens the awareness to higher ranges of experience, depth and intensity of sensitivity, and realization of identity with the cosmos by dropping of the false veils and bonds that limit the self.

This intimate sense of oneness of the self and the Universe is indeed a 'magical' way of looking at the world, as Tatyana Elizarenkova points out. But we must remember that the ancient concept of magic is not illusion, sleight of hand or trickery, but comes from the word Magi, which means wise men (similar to the Magi or sages from the East who visited Christ when he was born). This magic is what we may call a unitary way of thinking and seeing the world, discovering hidden powers of nature, and using or manipulating them, what is sometimes called white magic or occultism. But this magical way of thinking is intuitive, experimentally verified, childlike but not childish, and comes from great refinement and purity of the consciousness.

Sri Aurobindo notes in *The Secret of the Veda* that the identification of Indra as *Vrishabha* or the bull might have been the beginning of *Sankhya Darshana*. For Sankhya philosophy sees the Universe as *Purusha* and *Prakriti*, the male and the female, the two poles of Pure Consciousness and Manifest Energy.

Sri Aurobindo gives us another perspective on Sankhya philosophy in *The Human Cycle*, "...the Indian ideal of the relation between man and woman has always been governed by the symbolism of the relation between the Purusha and Prakriti (in the Veda *Nri* and *Gna*), the male and female divine Principles in the universe."

Swami Dayananda too in his exegesis, the *Rig Veda Bhasha Bhasya*, notes that Agni is the *vaachi* (speaker on behalf of, representative) of *Atman* and *Paramatman*, i.e., it represents the awareness of *Atman*. In other words, Agni represents the pure consciousness of *Purusha* or might be the seed for the later explorations of Sankhya. Indra then would represent the ascent of Agni to a higher level of consciousness, the luminous mind. The mind is then filled with *atma-prakaash* or the light of Pure Consciousness or *Purusha*.

Tantra in the Veda

In the *Rig Veda* X. 130.1, the world is seen as *tantu* or cloth, woven by Prajapati:

यो यज्ञो विश्वतस्तन्तुभिस्तत एकशतं देवकर्मेभिरायतः ।
इमे वयन्ति पितरो य आययुः प्र वयापं वयेत्यांसते ततै ॥

The ancient fathers weave, the yajna which is extended on every side by the threads. It is performed by the acts of gods, which are spread out in long time of over a hundred years. Weaving backwards and weaving forwards, the gods engaged in work, worship Prajapati in the vast world. (Translated by R.L. Kashyap)

Let us compare this with the definition of Tantra as offered by Mircea Eliade in his book *Yoga Immortality and Freedom*, "Among the many meanings of the word tantra (root *tan*, 'extend,' 'continue,' 'multiply') one concerns us particularly— that of 'succession,' 'unfolding,' 'continuous process.'"

Another etymology of Tantra is *tan-* plus *tra-*. *Tan-* represents weaving and *tra-* signifies liberation. Tantra is thus the freedom from interwoven threads of existence. Tatyana Elizarenkova in *Language and Style of the Vedic Rsis* translates *Tan-* as "to draw, to pull" (*a* + *tan-* "to stretch, to extend," "to pierce"). It seems obvious to me that the Tantra is present in the Veda at least inchoately if not in a fully developed form. I believe that the Vedic altar and its design influenced the later designs of the mandalas and yantras. And, of course, the mantra which is an integral part of Tantra is the perfection that Veda constantly aims for and achieves.

Finally, Vedanta, the highest summit of Vedic understanding, the peak, which is the fulfillment of the Vedic insight of true monism, the realization of *Tad Ekam*. And it seems to me that the monism of Veda became transformed to the non-duality of Vedanta. The realization of the highest consciousness of *Satyam-Ritam-Brihat* in the rishi paved way to a state where one's own self is not separate from the self of the Universe or those of other creatures.

Tatyana Elizarenkova says that a model of the universe should be interpreted as "a reduced and simplified reflection of the sum-total of all notions about the surrounding world that exist inside a given tradition and are regarded in their system-and-operation aspects." We can see how the notions of the rishis represented by what she called "sign-systems" affected the metaphysics, philosophies, and psychology of the Indian darshanas that followed the Veda. To this day, the Vedic model of the Universe continues in Indic darshanas in various forms.

Elizarenkova comments that, "the basic means of interpreting the Universe (in the Veda) is the myth." We should add that more than the myth, the basic means of interpreting the Universe for the Vedic rishis are sound, symbol, sense, and self. A profound sympathy and sensitivity to the world around is the secret to the rishis' model; however, this world is not just outside but also within. And this is the crucial difference between the Vedic and the modern scientific technical approaches. And the Vedic seers were as scientific, thorough, relentless, and fact-oriented, if not more than the researchers of today. And they created a corpus of knowledge that is still to be surpassed. Sri Aurobindo describes in his Foreword for *Hymns to the Mystic Fire*, "They discovered secrets and powers of Nature which were not those of the physical world but which could bring occult mastery over the physical world and physical things and to systematise this occult knowledge and power was also one of their strong preoccupations."

Elizarenkova also notes, "that the Vedic model of the Universe is cosmos-oriented. It is both a measure and a part of everything." It is true that the Vedic paradigm is cosmos-oriented, but to the rishis, the cosmos meant the inner and the outer worlds together seen from the vantage of a vision that was not only holistic but also transcendental. And this transcendence happens, as they discovered, when the consciousness is pure, unattached, liberated, non-directional, and free of all movements in a witness state.

And the world is always whole and complete, *poornamadah, poornamidam,* complete here and complete there, whether it is in chaos or cosmos. Each moment is perfect. Modern thought calls this synchrony. And as this wholeness evolves through the cycles of time, it is whole, perfect, and complete at each moment. This study of change over time is what is called diachrony. And

Elizarenkova adds, "Synchrony and diachrony are inseparably linked together (in the Veda); it is a salient feature of a mythopoetic model of the Universe." Here, her insight is remarkably precise and correct.

Thus, we see how most subsequent movements in Indian thought, philosophy, and spirituality have their starting points in the Veda. What is hinted at in the Veda, or is present in seed, grows into an entire system, complete in itself, autonomous, but retains its linkages consciously or unconsciously either with the Vedic framework or experience.

The Seven *Lokas*

As mentioned in the previous chapter, this whole Universe has many worlds in itself, dimensions within dimensions, layers within layers. It is not a flat abstract sameness but is exploding with variety and infinite possibility. The Vedic rishis described the various levels of existence as seven *lokas* or worlds. These *lokas* are a hierarchy of consciousness becoming increasingly subtler, refined, aware, effective, and unified as we move from the lowest to the highest. Ken Wilber calls this the "spectrum of consciousness" in his book by the same name. These *lokas* beginning from the dense state of matter evolved into life of plants and animals and then further into mind as in man. But this is not the end. For above the three *lokas* of matter, life and mind are higher strata and these have been termed the supramental by Sri Aurobindo, and above it the triune state of *sat-chit-ananda* or truth, consciousness, and bliss. Once we understand the seven *lokas* and see the ascent of being and awareness, the entire process of *yajna* and transformation begins to make sense. Perhaps modern scientists are attempting to resolve the inadequacy of just one *loka* to explain the paradoxes of existence by positing the concept of the multiverse. However, to contrast the two models, the multiverse refers to multiple or parallel universes as against the multiple dimensions within one Universe as described in the Veda.

We present the schema given to us by Sri Aurobindo in *The Doctrine of the Mystics*, to attempt to make this a bit easier to understand:

1. The supreme *sat-chit-ananda*	The triple divine worlds
2. The link-world supermind	The truth, right, and vast, manifested in *Swar* with its three luminous heavens
3. The triple lower world pure mind life-force matter	Heaven (*Dyaus*, the three heavens) The mid-region (*Antariksha*) Earth (the three earths)

Space is thus given multiple dimensions, such as *Antariksha*, literally the inner eye, which is equivalent to the realm of vital energies, or Vayu. Or *Dyau*, which is the realm of mind and home of the devas, the beings of light, and is ruled by Indra, the luminous mind. Or *Svara*, the vast expanse of Unity, that holds the consciousness of *Sacchidananda*, represented by Surya, the Sun. Or it is the *Parama Vyoma*, the Supreme Sky, where the rishi sees the mantra. Space is also coiled inside the *bila* or dark crypts in *adri*, or inconscient matter, where Indra discovers the rays of sunlight, the *gau*, with the help of *Sarama*, or the Divine intuition, and the mantra. Space is also the unique *Hiranyagarbha*, the golden womb, where everything is contained, *purna*, complete, and nothing exists outside its curve. There is no space that is outside the Universe, or that is absolute, since in all the Creation Hymns, it is created after the birth of the Universe has already been initiated by *Tad Ekam*, That One, or Prajapati, Vishvakarma, or the Purusha.

Similarly, time is not a linear movement that exists outside or is an eternal entity. It is cyclic and measured in yugas, the ages. Or it is a seed planted in the Inconscient that will fulfill its potential and its evolution or unfolding is the movement of time, or *Kaala*. Or it is the simultaneity of all events happening in the present, the now that is eternal, the *anant vartmana*, since all is complete at all times. This gave us the concept of time as *samaya*, literally being together or the right time. In this eternal present, every action is connected to the other integrally and intimately, and no happening may be excluded from the unity that upholds the actions taking place at each moment, what was later called the Co-Dependent Arising or *Pratitya Samutpada* in Vedanta and Buddhism. Time is thus a *chakra* or wheel, and its turning, the cycles of Sun and Soma, the biologic time of birth, aging and death. It is the blinking of an eye or infinitesimal moment; it is the recurrence of dawn and night, and the months and years. It is also the ending of "Time" in the "Timeless", as the Universe returns in *laya* to its origins, which is enacted every morning in the *yajna*. (Space and time are also discussed in chapter 11 with a slightly different nuance.)

The human is not only a being who inhabits the worlds of matter, life, and mind, he or she also lives in the higher states, although unaware of them. We may also say that all these seven *lokas* create the composite that is man. And the aspiration of the rishis in the Veda is to ascend from the lower three *lokas* (also known as *aparardha*) to the four *lokas* above; and they describe how they achieved this upward journey in Veda. These seven *lokas* are also descriptive of the outer world according to Veda since the outer is not separate from the inner.

The Veda also speaks of the *salilam apraketam* or the ocean of non-manifestation and what Sri Aurobindo called the Inconscient. This is the dense darkness that is even below matter since matter too has some level of awareness inherent in it, caused by the involution of *Sacchidananda* as it covers itself from itself. The Inconscient is the dense sea of complete absence of awareness that is created at the beginning of Creation by the Divine (variously named as *Hiranyagarbha, Purusha, Prajapati, Aditi,* etc.) and is described in Vedic Creation Hymns. Out of this unmanifest sea of total unconsciousness arises, first, the world of matter which evolves higher and higher into the other *lokas.* If this is understood, even Evolution begins to make sense as a coherent description that is not arbitrary as Charles Darwin thought *in The Origin of Species* or a conflict between matter and the Élan *Vital* as Henry Bergson philosophized in the *Creative Evolution.*

This helps us understand how the devas live in another *loka* and yet are always willing to help the rishi in his *yajna* as partners and collaborators; for they are aware of the inherent oneness shared by all and the universal movement of ascent or evolution in the cosmos on an individual and collective basis. This also helps us understand myths such as the birth of the seven Suns by Aditi (or the undivided consciousness who is the Mother of the devas), one for each *loka,* and the eighth one, *Martanda* or the dead egg, for the Inconscient. *Martanda* is also the Sun of the world of life and death, the dead seed that discovers life in the inconscient and becomes the Sun.

This also helps us see the mystic reality behind the myth of *Vala.* Since each *loka* is created by the Divine, and matter too is a manifestation of the Truth or the Divine, the Divine can be discovered, lived, expressed, and manifested even in the darkest densest states of physical awareness. And when Indra with the help of Sarama, as noted earlier, recovers the hidden Sunlight or *gau* from deep inside the darkest recesses or *bila* of matter, it is a profound symbol of the rishi discovering the Divine consciousness even in his physical body. As C.G. Jung noted in his studies of alchemy, the quest for transformation is an ancient human ideal. This transformation, usually misunderstood, is not just an attempt to change base metal into gold, but the base matter of our bodies into golden light.

If we understand the hierarchy of the seven *lokas*, then the myth of *Vritra* also makes sense. For Indra who is the luminous mind is obstructed by *Vritra* from allowing his light to flow down to the lower *lokas*. With the help of Sarasvati or the Divine Inspiration, he strikes down *Vritra* with his *vajra* or thunderbolt of lightning and revelation. This allows the waters blocked by *Vritra* to descend to the lower hemisphere or *aparardha*, bringing the Divine light and knowledge to the human mind, vital, and body. What does this mean for mankind today? That we need to remove the obstacles in our mentality to the higher functions which are possible to it. To see the limitations imposed on us by our own ignorance and darkness and allow our awareness to grow luminous by the fullest presence of Indra. To invoke our highest potential of mind and be open to letting go of our mental blocks.

Another corollary of seeing the world as a multi-dimensional and many-layered representation of One Reality is that every plane is not only a just expression of the Divine but is the Divine. That is why we see that in the Veda, there is a sense of the sacred in everything that a human does. The *yajna* is a profound connection with the cosmos and giving up of oneself to the divine. It is an ecosystemic and holistic, non-zero-sum thought process (such that we can appreciate now in our troubled modern times of global warming, soil depletion and the gathering dangers of pollutants, waste, plastic, and radiation in our natural resources each of which is a deva).

Vedic Oneness and Spirituality

Another critically significant feature of this model, as discussed earlier, is what may be called Vedic Non-Dualism and the Vedic state of Non-Differentiation. The same unity is described eloquently in several verses throughout the Veda where it uses terms such as *Tad Ekam*, That One, *Tad Satyam*, That Truth, or

Tad Adbhutam, That Mystery. This is the first time in human history that a clear, organized, and systematic articulation of the One Reality has been made, which later went on to impact all the future religions and denominations. But this Vedic Oneness and Monism is not against the multiplicity and the unique nature of each individual manifestation in the cosmos, it respects both and celebrates the diversity. This respect of multiplicity is ordinarily confused as polytheism, which is not the right understanding of the Vedic way of life (more on this in chapter 6).

The key to understanding the Veda is to see it as a spiritual description of the experiences of highly evolved men and women, who at a certain stage of human history were born on earth and helped prepare it for the next age. These men and women, called rishis and kavis, were not dealing with abstractions, metaphysics, or concepts. They simply described what they saw and lived. And their awareness was refined enough that they could see beyond what most mortals could barely conceive of. Thus, they did not think; they saw and they heard with an evolved and elevated awareness. That is why, it is said that they saw the mantras and heard the Revelation, and they did not write out of a human effort. The rishis are not thinkers, they are seers. The kavis are not versifiers, they are seer-poets, who can see through and beyond and reveal that in a body of sound that can transmit their experience to the listener who is open and receptive.

According to the Veda, the human being has the power to grow and ascend to a level higher than even the gods—to become a deva oneself, as the Greek aspiration used to be, but here made practical and experiential. With a highly sophisticated system, that could be universally applied, experimented with, researched, validated, and lived, the Vedic seers gave us an extremely important document and legacy that we can always be grateful for and proud of. The whole Vedic model of the

Universe is one that sees tremendous potential in each human, to such an extent that each of us can not only tap the power of the Universe but manifest it in various ways.

The Truth of the Universe

Another critical key to this model is the realization that there is an eternal truth beyond this world of change and death. This is what the ancient rishis discovered. That we can find this Truth and there is a path for it, *ritasya panthah*. And not only can we find this Truth or *Ritam*, but we can also live it in our human state and even in physical awareness. And by realizing and establishing it in our awareness, sharing the joys of it, purifying ourselves in its Fire and Light, Agni, we could find the secret of immortality, the bliss that can metamorphose our human lot. This bliss is the nectar of *amritam*, the *Somarasa* that the rishis sought after and extracted from their own bodies and selves by living a highly purified life and state.

And then they also discovered that not only can one live this Truth, one can also share it with the power of the mantra and meditation, self-surrender and offering to the Divine within and without. And that using the name and mantra for a deva gave them the power over the deva to invoke it and facilitate its action on earth. Joel P. Brereton and Stephanie W. Jamison in *The Rigveda: A Guide* call this the speech act. That the inspired 'spoken word (is an) extraordinary compulsive force.'

The legend of fighting obstructers and obscurers, manipulators, and devils, *Vala* and *Vrika*, Panis and *Dasyus*, is another aspect of their model that is today part of all the religions. These forces of ignorance and darkness essentially may be seen as negative from the human perspective. But from the supramental perspective, they have their own place in the universal becoming and manifestation of *Ritam*, and to help humans realize their deficiencies and overcome them.

This model of the Universe is not that far-fetched and can be seen to have affected our modern life and thought, religions and theology even today. We have the concept of a transcendental Truth or Reality, or God. We have the polarity of God and the Devil or *Diablo* in the Abrahamic religions and *Mara* in other *Nastik* thought dharmic systems such as Buddhism. Zoroastrians too have the *Ahura Mazda* and *Ahiraman*.

Strange as it may sound, the asura or the devil can also mean the powerful one and the term may be used for devas too. But then, the Vedic system does not relegate any aspect of the Universe to eternal rejection or eternal hell. For every power of the cosmos is here to aid us in our journey and growth in its becoming.

The Composite Reality of Man

The Vedic sense of the Self of man is a composite of various levels, and so is its idea of the place of mankind in the world. The human self has all the potential inherent in its body, mind, heart, and vital that is anywhere present in the universe and the human can access it if the secret could somehow be found. The Veda gives us that secret: it is through the power of sound and the mantra, the power of self-surrender and offering to the Divine and invoking the Divine, the power of concentrating one's mind and being and making it luminous, discovering the secret of bliss in life and growing in inspiration, intuition, knowledge, jnana, and therefore, reaching a higher level and force of action. These tools later grew into various branches such as Yoga, Sankhya, Vedanta, Bhakti, Advaita, etc., but the secret came from the Veda.

As Sri Aurobindo elaborates in *Hymns to the Mystic Fire*,

The preoccupation of the Mystics was with self-knowledge and a profounder world-knowledge; they found out that in man there was a deeper self and inner being behind the surface of the outward physical man, which it was his highest business to discover and know. "Know thyself" was their great precept, just as in India to know the Self, the Atman became the great spiritual need, the highest thing for the human being.

How to find the *Ritasya Panthah* or the Path of Truth?

How is the human going to discover *Ritam*? According to Veda, there are several possible approaches. One is discovering the Agni and by invoking it. This discovery is the Divine within us. This Agni is discovered by the right use of inspired speech and finding in its sounds the *beej dhvanis* and mantra, symbolic action or ritual, surrender and self-offering to the Divine. It is strengthened by refining one's thought and enunciation, by growing the Flame and Light within; and by discovering Soma, the joy of being and living. The *tejas* of Agni changes the body's physiology, which generates bliss, by holding this Soma in the heart, and using it to transform the vital and mind, and by raising the mind to the higher level of Indra or luminous mind. Until the seeker finds and identifies with the Sun as his or her own secret reality and highest consciousness. To discover *Bhadram* and *Svadha*, the divine benevolence and goodwill and harmony with all.

The Agni is the quiet still voice and awareness that is always within us as an eye in the heart, a point of joy through the worst of vicissitudes. Sri Aurobindo called this Agni the Psychic Being in his darshana. This psychic is our true self, the *anahata*, the *chaitya purusha*, the *hrdi purusha*, and the *jeeva atman*. And its true nature is Divine and the Light itself. It has within it all the knowledge of the worlds, and our lives. It is the purifier and the invoker, the leader and the enjoyer of bliss, the child and the messenger, and the deliverer and the guardian of our truth.

What are the other clues to reach the Truth according to the
Veda? Invoke the Agni and offer it *Ghritam*, which is not just
purified butter but a luminous clear dense mind. When such a
state is offered to the Divine within, there is rapid growth in the
blaze of the fire in *yajna*.

Another hint is to ascend Indra. As we grow in our cognitive
abilities, and let the mind grow more refined and capable of
thought that is deeper, higher, and wider, the mental awareness
can grow closer to the Light of Surya. Or is filled with *atma-
prakasha*, the Light of the Self, if we use the term used in later
Sankhya traditions.

Surya is the other end of Agni in the Vedic model and is
a form of Agni—the symbol of unity and *Sacchidananda*, the
Supermind as Sri Aurobindo calls it. This dynamic will and *chitta*
when invoked transforms our lives in the mind, the vital and the
physical, and as Sri Aurobindo showed, also the Inconscient. In
the verses of the Veda and Sri Aurobindo, we learn that higher
mentality and enlightened consciousness form a continuum and
are not pitted against one another.

These are the hints to the golden path each of which was
developed by later darshanas into gigantic systems of pragmatics
and application, as spontaneous out-branchings and elaborations.

This in brief is the Vedic 'model of the Universe.' A highly
evolved and sophisticated system, it created a great literature and
culture around it, and built the grounds for the next age: the
age of the intellect which finds it hard to understand it now, yet
without the Veda could not have possibly come into being. It
has justly been called a kaleidoscope where time past and time
future begin to change with the actions of the present, which fits
in appropriately with its model of spiral, multidimensional, and
cyclic time.

It seems to be the framework out of which the *astika* traditions
(i.e., those that accept the authority of the Veda) arose. There is
much we can learn from this paradigm as we can see it evolve

differently in the various darshanas like Sankhya, Tantra, Vedanta, Bhakti, among others. In Sankhya, it becomes dualistic with an analytic enumerative approach of the various tattvas or essences of the world. In Tantra, it focuses on the world of manifestation and studies its inner unity, processes and eventually, its vast intelligence that is both galactic and microscopic at the same time. In Vedanta, it moves to the complete unity, culminating in the non-duality of existence, Advaita. In the Bhakti movements, it takes different forms in the Vaishnava, Shaivite, and Shakta movements with the worship of Vishnu, Shiva, and Shakti as the highest Personality of That indescribable Reality, *Tad Ekam*. And Subhash Kak has shown in *The Idea of India: Bharat as a Civilisation* that even Buddhism adopted the Vedic model of the Universe without accepting its rituals.

We may see this model recur in the pre-Socratic philosophers. Thales with his insistence that the Universe originated from water brings us back to the *Salilam Apraketam*, though we are not certain if this is due to Vedic influences. Parmenides with his One reality reminds us of *Tad Ekam* again, That One. Plato with his world of Idea behind the imperfect world we live in recalls the *lokas* of the *parardha*, the levels above the *Svara*, where the Idea is not just a concept, but has the power of manifestation inherent in it, what Sri Aurobindo calls the Real-Idea.

Similarly, Hegel in his grand Synthesis of the Universe brings us back to the unity that the Vedic rishis remind us of in almost every mandala of the Veda. Arthur Schopenhauer, it is said, danced on the streets when he first read of Vedanta, for it said clearly, according to him, what he had spent his entire life attempting to articulate.

The Vedic model of the Universe is alive with us today, whether in movies (such as *The Matrix* or *2001, the Space Odyssey*, or *Star Wars*), or the poetry of T.S. Eliot or the psychological concepts of Carl G. Jung. It comes back to us in various motifs and symbols when we study the science of signs or Semiology.

And it is worth reflecting on when we attempt to understand other models of the Universe offered to us by modern sciences, to not only contrast with but perhaps even augment the new insights into artificial intelligence and physics that attempt to study consciousness and its relationship with the world.

III

The Unique Non-dualism of the Veda

6

The Veda and the History of Oneness and *Sarvata*

One of the earliest articulations of the Oneness of existence in human history was made in the *Rig Veda*.

Modern scholarship and popular fiction has presumed that the Unity of the Universe is a prerogative of later religions, and was discovered by them. That the so-called religion of Hinduism, polytheistic, pantheistic, at best, reached a confused disunity, or at best a semblance of Unity, among various gods termed Henotheism by Max Mueller.

Nothing could be further from the truth. The oldest scriptural literature available in entirety today is the Veda. And as T.V. Kapali Shastri has shown with multiple references from each mandala of the Veda that the One Reality, *Tad Ekam* or *Ekam Sat*, is constantly described and shown as the truth behind all the diverse phenomena of the world.

Sri Aurobindo has famously translated *Rig Veda* V.62.1 in *Hymns to the Mystic Fire* as a clear depiction of monotheism in the hymns, which was picked up by *Isha Upanishad* shloka 16 and became a part of its Vedanta,

> In connection with the symbol of the Sun a notable and most significant verse in a hymn of the fifth Mandala … shows not only the profound mystic symbolism of the Vedic poets, but also how the writers of the Upanishads understood the *Rig Veda* and justifies their belief in the inspired knowledge of their forerunners.

"There is a Truth covered by a Truth," runs the Vedic passage, "where they unyoke the horses of the Sun; the ten hundred stood together, there was That One; I saw the greatest (best, most glorious) of the embodied gods." Then mark how the seer of the Upanishad translates this thought or this mystic experience into his own later style, keeping the central symbol of the Sun, but without any secrecy in the sense. Thus runs the passage in the Upanishad,

> The face of the Truth is covered with a golden lid, O Pushan, that remove for the vision of the law of the Truth. O Pushan (fosterer), sole seer, O Yama, O Sun, O Child of the Father of beings, marshal and gather together thy rays; I see the Light which is that fairest (most auspicious) form of thee; he who is this *Purusha*, He am I.

These passages show a clear cognition of the One Reality that is also the Reality of one's own existence, individually. Sri Aurobindo further explains,

> The Sun in both the passages, as constantly in the Veda and frequently in the Upanishad, is the Godhead of the supreme Truth and Knowledge and his rays are the light emanating from that supreme Truth and Knowledge. It is clear from this instance—and there are others—that the seer of the Upanishad had a truer sense of the meaning of the ancient Veda than the mediaeval ritualistic commentator (Sayana) with his gigantic learning, much truer than the modern and very different mind of the European scholars.

The One Truth of the Veda

M.P. Pandit in *Selected Works of M.P. Pandit* contradicts S. Radhakrishnan's statement that when 'the half-gods of the Veda die, the true God arrives.' He notes that there are several *riks* in the *Rig Veda* extolling the One Godhead as the Source and Origin of all the Gods, the Deity of deities:

For instance:

1) *Ekam sad viprah bahudha vadanti*
   The One Existent, the illumined call variously. (*Rig Veda* I.164.46)

2) *Ejad dhruvam patyate vishvamekam charat patadi vishunu vijatam*
   The Universal One that rules over the mobile and the fixed (is) what walks, what flies, what is this manifold birth. (*Rig Veda* III.54.8)

3) *Mahat devanam asuratvamekam*
   The powerful Might of the Gods is the Great One. (*Rig Veda* III.55.1)

4) *Vishve devah samanasah saketa ekam kritumabhi vi yanti sadhu...*
   All the Gods with a single mind, a common intuition, move aright in their divergent paths towards the One Will. (*Rig Veda* VI.9.5)

5) *Ekam va idam vibabhuva sarvam*
   The One has become All this. (*Rig Veda* VIII.58.2)

6) *Yo devanam namdha ek eva ...*
   One who alone is the holder of the Names of all the Gods. (*Rig Veda* X.82.3)

7) *Suparna viprah kavyo vayobhih ekam santam bahudha kalpayanti*
   The One Existent, beautiful of plumage, the illumined seers by the words formulate in many ways (or forms). (*Rig Veda* X.114.5)

Vedic Unity

In recent times, it was Swami Dayananda who first brought us back to this fact of literature, religion, and history. Sri

Aurobindo confirmed this with his various translations of the
Srutis, the Veda, Upanishads, and the Gita. The Unity in the
Veda is clear, precise, and articulated firmly throughout, but it is
not oppressive, rigid, flat or abstract. This Vedic Unity creates an
interplay of monotheism, monism, pantheism, and panentheism
on the ground of a single Reality and has no struggle with
polytheism. Whether we disagree on when and how it precisely
originated, it should be universally accepted that it is indeed our
first record of diverse spiritual experiences.

As noted, this Unity is not the monotheism as is understood by
the West or later religions in the Abrahamic tradition. Nor is it the
monism that took birth in Western thought in the 18th century
after Baruch Spinoza. The God of Old Testament can be irascible
and prone to anger, recriminations, or jealousy. The theology of
the New Testament is saved by the spirituality of Jesus rather than
a sound and rational framework of thought. Later religions are
often plagued by a misconception of God as an anthropomorphic
'schoolmaster of souls,' as Blake had exclaimed. Vedic *Sarvata*
sees all existence as One Reality and Truth, which manifests
innumerably, multitudinously, and with infinite diversity. There is
no separate God sitting somewhere in the heavens.

A clear-eyed realization and acceptance of this truth shows
how the Indic civilization was not only far ahead of its time,
refined and mature in thought and realization, but also that the
understanding of Monism and Monotheism is extremely poor in
several later developments in religion and theology. The duality
of God and Satan in Western traditions does not make sense,
nor does an eternal hell.

For a mature theology it may still be worthwhile to rediscover
the Oneness and Non-Dualism of the Veda, its nuanced
understanding and vision arising from spiritual confirmation,
not imaginary projections of our greed and fear.

What is this Oneness or Unity of Veda? The Veda is clear.
There is One Reality called by the sages differently. This One
Reality is not a static or siloed entity, but is dynamic, alive,

immanent, but also cosmic and transcendent. Its various energies and manifestations are called devas by the Veda.

The devas in Veda are not fear-mongers. Nor do they seek to punish humans who wish to ascend above them. Rather they facilitate individual growth and ascent as active partners full of *bhadram*, auspiciousness, and good will, *Svasti*.

The devas are psychological and spiritual forces of the world who do not create fear or retribution but are the source of light, wisdom, immortality, and truth. Without them there is no spiritual victory of the seeker, for they are integral constituents of his or her inner life. If approached with purity, love, harmony, and self-surrender, they are sure to be the guardians and protectors of the pilgrim seekers and adepts. Also, the devas can come together and become one deva, called *Vishvadeva* in Veda, who combines all their diverse powers into One being again. *Vishvadeva* literally means all-devas and is invoked in various mantras as the One Deva who brings all the diverse manifestations of the One Reality back into one being closer to the seeker and who can be invoked by the *yajna*.

The Hidden Connections of Unity

We see a similar sense of Unity behind the various descriptions of Surya. Surya deva in Veda has many forms and manifestations, as described by Tatyana Elizarenkova in the *Language and Style of the Vedic Rsis*. He is *Pushana*, the nourisher, 'who gives prosperity to people, cattle and pastures.' And *Savitar*, the Impeller, the Inciter. He is *Mitra*, 'the god of friendship and contract as well as of Sun and light.' He is *Ushas*, or the goddess of dawn. And he is Agni in all its forms. According to Sri Aurobindo, Surya Deva or Sun God is the symbol of our highest unity or *Sacchidananda*, as noted earlier in this chapter.

As we study the various aspects or emanations of Surya Deva in Veda, we begin to sense the fluid and flexible mind and consciousness of the wise rishis who helped create it. And it might puzzle us too how a single deva can become another and then return to itself without contradiction. And if Surya is Agni in all its manifestations, it means Surya is right here burning in our hearts! And in the rocks and waters and our *yajna*, our gut (as *jathar-agni*) or in our desires (*kama-agni*) and even our cells.

This is a reverse of the morphology seen when we study the evolution of Agni, for Agni as it is invoked, rises to become Mitra-Varuna and then Indra, and eventually Surya itself. And this chiasmatic approach confirms in code that it is the same energy or *Urja* sustaining the whole Universe and each deva is inherently connected and related to the other, through its very nature and reality.

Such is the intense Unity of the Veda that it does not need to struggle with the concept of an eternal hell, like the later religions do. For an eternal hell in Vedic thought is a contradiction in terms. Divine love cannot create a punishment for all time for his own creation. Divine Oneness or *Ekam Sat*, is not separate or antagonistic to the rishi or humanity but in essence and realization is one with him too, just like with all creation.

The Sense of the Non-Dual and the Only

Thus, a non-dual approach to life is the hallmark of Vedic thought that fully flowers in Advaita or non-dual Vedanta. Seeing a hidden unity throughout the Universe and its countless manifestations is essential to understanding the Veda and eventually ourselves. This is the essential paradigm, breathtaking in its simplicity, yet fluid enough to entertain all possible varieties and possibilities that life offers. This non-dual worldview is what helped later darshanas develop the mighty and unitary understanding of Advaita Vedanta, one of the highest achievements of mankind.

And this non-duality of vision too manifested as the *Kaivalyam* or the Onliness that is described in several Upanishads, such as the *Kaivalya, Amrtabindu,* and *Muktika.* In the third chapter of *Shvetashwatara Upanishad,* the term *Kevalah* is brought out in the sense of the Absolute.

यदाऽतमस्तान्न दिवा न रात्रिः
    न सन्नचासच्छिव एव केवलः ।
तदक्षरं तत् सवितुर्वरेण्यं
    प्रज्ञा च तस्मात् प्रसृता पुराणी ॥ १८ ॥

When darkness is not and day dawneth not nor night cometh, nor reality nor unreality, but all is Shiva, the Blessed One pure and absolute, that verily is the Imperishable and the Sun, more glorious than Savita and from Him Wisdom, the Ancient Goddess, was poured in the beginning. (Translated by Sri Aurobindo)

We can see the influences of the first mantra of *Nasadiya Sukta* in *Rig Veda* X.129.1 in this passage:

नासदासीन्नो सदासीत्तदानीम् नासीद्रजो नो व्योमा परो यत् ।
किमावरीवः कुह कस्य शर्मन्नंभः किमासीद्गहनं गभीरम् ॥ १ ॥

Non-existence then was not, nor Existence, neither the principle of movement, nor space there beyond. What covered over all and where, or what was any resting-place? What were the waters? Fathomless abyss? (Translated by R.L. Kashyap)

And we also see the influence of the *Gayatri Mantra* (*Rig Veda* III.62.10) on the shloka on *Kevalah* in the *Shwetashwatara,* with the invocation of *Savitur* or the Impeller (*Saviturvarenyam*). *Muktika Upanishad* describes *Kaivalya* as the highest form of liberation possible to an adept. We also see the concept of *Kaivalya* in Jainism where it is the highest attainment of wisdom

possible to the soul. And *Shoonya* seems to me to be an extension
again of the first mantra of *Nasadiya Sukta*, where all features are
stripped away to give us a sense of the ultimate reality.

We can see not only the profound influence of Veda as
reference in Upanishads directly quoted by them, but also an
extension of its symbols and concepts into a formulation of
what became the glorious understanding of Vedanta seen in the
Upanishads and even Buddhism.

7

Vedic Vedanta and Its Re-emergence

All life is Yoga, proclaimed Sri Aurobindo. And with this statement he once more turned the nation and its darshana to the Vedic paradigm of encompassing all aspects of human life. The Veda, a life-affirming integral approach to existence, has been forgotten by the Indian mind for a couple of millennia at least. When the Buddha established his first precept that the nature of *samsara* is suffering or *dukkha*, he had veered away from the Vedic and Vedantic ideal of *poornta* in spirituality, for in Veda, the world is not *dukkha samsara*, and all is a manifestation of the secret Oneness, *Tad Ekam*.

For, the moment one calls the nature of the world to be sorrow, one has created a schism in one's embrace of life. Sankara was erroneously understood to be calling the world an illusion, Maya, and recommending renunciation of life to take *sannyasa*. Veda itself was deemed to be external and propitiatory rituals by the *Mimansaks* and interpreters like Sayana, and its inner symbolism, slowly forgotten by its practitioners.

It was Swami Vivekananda who stated that *dvaitavada*, *vishisht advaita*, and *advaita* Vedanta were only different aspects and stages of the same realization. This was in accordance with his guru Sri Ramakrishna's experiences that all the various religions and *panthas*, including Vaishnava Bhakti, Tantra, Advaita Vedanta, Buddhism, Islam, Christianity, etc., came from the same Divine source. Sri Aurobindo advanced it further by proclaiming that all these were influenced by the same Vedic source that came before them. The keynote here in returning to

Veda or and the Vedic paradigm is the integrality with which Sri Aurobindo embraced all the various *darshanas* and *panthas* and brought them into a Unitary Vision that gave each difference its due importance.

In his own *advaitik* realization of Narayana in Alipore Jail in 1908, Sri Aurobindo saw all reality as One, the Narayana and Vasudeva, who was not only the entire objective world but also intimately his own subjective existence too,

> I looked at the jail that secluded me from men and it was no longer by its high walls that I was imprisoned; no, it was Vasudeva who surrounded me. I walked under the branches of the tree in front of my cell, but it was not the tree, I knew it was Vasudeva, it was Srikrishna whom I saw standing there and holding over me His shade. I looked at the bars of my cell, the very grating that did duty for a door and again I saw Vasudeva. It was Narayana who was guarding and standing sentry over me. Or I lay on the coarse blankets that were given me for a couch and felt the arms of Srikrishna around me, the arms of my Friend and Lover. This was the first use of the deeper vision He gave me.

In the chapter on the Vedic model of the Universe, we have discussed how the rishis felt a deep sense of oneness with the whole world and all its creatures. Sri Aurobindo gives us the same unity in his own direct manner. And how this unity is a lived and realized experience that transforms the experiencer fundamentally and forever.

He added,

> I looked at the prisoners in the jail, the thieves, the murderers, the swindlers, and as I looked at them I saw Vasudeva, it was Narayana whom I found in these darkened souls and misused bodies. Amongst these thieves

and dacoits there were many who put me to shame by their sympathy, their kindness, the humanity triumphant over such adverse circumstances. Once more He spoke to me and said, "Behold the people among whom I have sent you to do a little of my work. This is the nature of the nation I am raising up and the reason why I raise them."

Here we see the same merging of *bhakti* and *jnana* as we have seen in the *Agni Sukta*, Mantras 7 and 9. And this devotion-knowledge translates into a different kind of action, from a different source, with a different poise, and to lasting effect. And that is true Karma Yoga. The bondages of anxiety, ambition, desire, anger, greed, pride, attachment, and fear are gone.

Sri Aurobindo reached the radical realization that is taken as the summit of *adhyatma* in traditional Yoga. He heard and saw the *Tad Ekam* that the rishi had described in *Rig Veda* V.62.1 before he knew that it had already been delineated in those mantras of antiquity.

I looked at the Prosecuting Counsel and it was not the Counsel for the prosecution that I saw; it was Srikrishna who sat there, it was my Lover and Friend who sat there and smiled. "Now do you fear?" He said, "I am in all men and I overrule their actions and their words. My protection is still with you and you shall not fear… I am in the nation and its uprising and I am Vasudeva, I am Narayana, and what I will, shall be, not what others will. What I choose to bring about, no human power can stay."

This may perhaps be considered as Sri Aurobindo's own *Vishvaroop Darshana* of Narayana akin to the one mentioned in the Gita, Chapter 11, beheld by Arjuna.

This mystical insight into the nature of the universe as the Divine and only the Divine is crucial to any understanding of

Vedic monism. For, as noted, the Vedic rishis did not arrive at the unity of the cosmos through an effort of thought but a felt, loved, and lived oneness of existence. This is the true basis of all Veda and Vedanta. And the Unity discussed in the prior chapter is but a by-product of this identification with the One Reality, called Narayana by Sri Aurobindo (among countless other yogis in the Sanatana tradition) and *Tad Ekam* by the Vedic rishis.

(We should perhaps addend here that *anubhava* or, the inner experience, is the foundation of the Vedic way of life—not textuality or scriptural authority. Sri Ramakrishna, once again, foreground the experience of self-realization as the basis of Hinduism. Vivekananda called it practical Vedanta. Ramana taught through silence, which in *Dakshinamurti stotram* is considered the highest form of speech. Sri Aurobindo's realization too became the basis of his understanding, and not the other way round. Veda proclaims *brahmavid brahmaiva bhavati*—the knowner of Brahman becomes Brahman.)

This too is the basis of the clear message of the first line of the *Isha Upanishad*:

Isha vasyam idam sarvam yad kinch jagatyam jagat
(All this is the inhabitation of the Lord, whatever moves in this Universe.)

This too is the basis of the grand vision of the Gita in the Chapter 11, where Sri Krishna shows Arjuna his *Vishwaroop*, or Universal Being. And the basis of Sri Krishna's exhortation to Arjuna to follow his dharma and fight the enemy of righteousness, for in his vision all is the Divine, whether in work or *jnana*, or *bhakti*. Nothing is excluded from the Unity, whether the external world of action or even the world of war.

We see that the Vedic model of the Universe has begun translating into different expressions of the same intuitive knowledge, *vijnana*, that the rishis had experienced. And often the Vedic symbology recurs in the Upanishads and Gita with the same hidden significances.

For example, in the *Kena Upanishad*, Agni and Indra return along with other devas in the third part. And in the Gita, the symbol of the *yajna* comes back powerfully using the same integral integrating paradigm.

ब्रह्मार्पणं ब्रह्म हविर्ब्रह्माग्नौ ब्रह्मणा हुतम् |
ब्रह्मैव तेन गन्तव्यं ब्रह्मकर्मसमाधिना ||4.24||

Brahman is the giving, Brahman is the food-offering, by Brahman it is offered into the Brahman-fire. Brahman is that which is to be attained by Samadhi in Brahman-action. (Translated by Sri Aurobindo)

When any *pantha* (path) or lineage veers away to an exclusive approach, either emphasizing one aspect of life over another or rejecting one or deprecating it, the whole integrality of Veda and Vedanta is missed and forgotten. Thus, it was that when the Buddha emphasized Nirvana over *samsara*, or when Sankara explained that the *jagat* is *mithya* and only Brahman is the Truth, the understanding of Vedanta took on a siloed paradigm. This impacted the vitality and brainpower of India, as *sannyasa* became the ideal for the highest and the best and a sense of rejecting the world of phenomena the greatest precept.

It seems to me that Swami Dayananda, when he railed against the various *panthas*, was saying the same thing, that the *poorna* or integral Vedanta had been restricted and made partial. It was up to Sri Aurobindo to correct this deviation of the Indian spiritual mind and bring it back to the original impetus and inspiration of the Veda; that all is the Divine, nothing is excluded, nothing is outside. And the physical and material is as much the creation of the One Reality as the highest state of consciousness is in its equal but equally discerning vision.

Sri Aurobindo in *The Life Divine* shows that the ascetic ideal and the materialist denial of God are the two tendencies that miss out on the true essence of the Universe and its true unity. Only once we have accepted matter too as the fit manifestation of the Lord can the contradictions of thought, feeling and life be resolved, the theories of evolution and the symbolism of Veda presented in the light of a higher reason and insight.

In philosophy as in poetry, Sri Aurobindo brought us back to the Vedic paradigm and restated what he called Universal Realism as against a Universal Illusionism. The *Satyam-Ritam-Brihat* of the Veda is the unitary consciousness of the Truth that is vast, and master of its dynamic will and action. It is called the "Supermind" by Sri Aurobindo or the Truth-Consciousness, the *Rit-Chit* of the Veda. The Veda was the first stirring of Yoga and spirituality in humanity. But it is not just a historical record, since its achievements are still worthy of being recovered and studied for humanity's evolution. Its vast and integral vision can still help reconcile the various *panthas* that have emerged from it into a harmonious co-existence and perhaps cooperation.

In the Veda, Surya, or the symbol of the Supermind, is also Agni, the Divine in the heart, or what Sri Aurobindo called the Psychic Being. And this again underlines the hidden unity of the individual divinity and cosmic Divine, and creates the metaphysical basis for later Upanishadic revelations.

The Supramental consciousness works through various strata of the mind, termed Overmind, Intuitive Mind, Illumined Mind, and Higher Mind by Sri Aurobindo. And as the revelation of Supramental Truth is seen by the mind of the rishi, he may see flashes of inspiration like lightning or the thunderbolt or *Vajra* (of Indra) in the Veda. Or he may ascend to a Luminous state of mind, where knowledge is constantly known in an enlightened or illumined state of consciousness, called Indra by the Veda. And it is Indra, the living power or Deva of the Illumined Mind, who removes all obstructions of understanding or mental constructs and opens up the floodgates of inspiration from above. This is the previously noted legend of *Vritra*, the obstruction of mental knowledge and wisdom, whom Indra destroys with his thunderbolt, aided by Sarasvati, the Devi of supramental sight and inspiration.

Thus the legend of *Vala*, where guided by *Sarama* or Intuition Indra recovers the Rays of Sun or *Gau* that have been hidden in matter by *Vala*. For the *Gau* hidden in matter's cave is the Supramental Knowledge and light hidden in the darkest recesses of matter or the inconscient, and recovering that truth is one of ideals and aspirations of the Vedic rishi. Since they saw even matter as a fit instrument of the One Reality, in which the highest consciousness was involved and buried and could be awakened and liberated with the power of an integral Yoga and *yajna*.

In this light, we can also understand the principle of Evolution, not as propounded by Charles Darwin as a matter of chance, or by Henri Bergson as the movement of *Élan Vital* or Life Force but in the Vedic and Vedantic perspective, the hidden Supramental consciousness in the inconscient ascending upward through life and mind along the ladder or 'spectrum' of consciousness. The Vedantic approach towards evolution is the movement of wholeness towards wholeness, infinite to infinite, in a plethora of forms and appearances, in a higher and greater organization of form and spirit. It is not random nor a conflict between the duality of life and matter. (Evolution has also been discussed in Chapter 5 with a different slant.)

Thus, Evolution becomes a consistent inevitable theory, and not a contradiction in terms, nor a paradox, if we apply to it the knowledge gleaned from the Veda. Explaining all this in a larger darshana, Sri Aurobindo opened up the world of metaphysics and philosophy to Veda and Vedanta. Modern philosophers such as Ken Wilber have continued his work in integrating knowledge, psychology, philosophy, and even physics, and this has been a direct impact of Sri Aurobindo in bringing back the Vedic truths to the modern mind.

The Vedic model of the Universe, its organization, symbology, poetics, and sound-structure gives consistency and coherence to all the Indian darshanas to follow. And creates the non-dual understanding that forms the bedrock of Vedanta. For the non-dual or *advaita* is the next step for a consciousness steeped in Vedic monism. This same hidden interweaving singleness creates the basis for later Tantra, which Sri Aurobindo integrated with Vedanta in his Integral Philosophy, thus taking us back to the original Vedic divination of a man's relationship with the world.

8

Vedic Realizations of the Mother and Sri Aurobindo

An Early Vedic Experience

In a letter by Mirra Alfassa, the Mother of Sri Aurobindo Ashram, to Sri Aurobindo an extraordinary spiritual experience is related. And it is instructive to read it along with Sri Aurobindo's comments on it, for they shed an important light not only on the experience but also his own insightful view. And shows the remarkable difference between the original Vedic worldview, which was integral and did not see the material world and the earth as separate from an all-embracing spirituality.

We excerpt the letter here in full, for it is an important document of one of the greatest spiritual figures of last century (dated November 26, 1915, translated by Sri Aurobindo or revised and published under his guidance):

The entire consciousness immersed in divine contemplation, the whole being enjoyed a supreme and vast felicity.

Then was the physical body seized, first in its lower members and next the whole of it, by a sacred trembling which made all personal limits fall away little by little even in the most material sensation. The being grew in greatness progressively, methodically, breaking down every barrier, shattering every obstacle, that it might contain and manifest a force and a power which increased ceaselessly in

immensity and intensity. It was as a progressive dilatation
of the cells until there was a complete identification with
the earth: the body of the awakened consciousness was the
terrestrial globe moving harmoniously in ethereal space.
And the consciousness knew that its global body was thus
moving in the arms of the universal Being, and it gave itself,
it abandoned itself to It in an ecstasy of peaceful bliss. Then
it felt that its body was absorbed in the body of the universe
and one with it; the consciousness became the consciousness
of the universe, immobile in its totality, moving infinitely in
its internal complexity. The consciousness of the universe
sprang towards the Divine in an ardent aspiration, a perfect
surrender, and it saw in the splendour of the immaculate
Light the radiant Being standing on a many-headed serpent
whose body coiled infinitely around the universe. The
Being in an eternal gesture of triumph mastered and created
at one and the same time the serpent and the universe that
issued from him; erect on the serpent he dominated it with
all his victorious might, and the same gesture that crushed
the hydra enveloping the universe gave it eternal birth.
Then the consciousness became this Being and perceived
that its form was changing once more; it was absorbed into
something which was no longer a form and yet contained
all forms, something which, immutable, sees—the Eye, the
Witness. And what It sees, is. Then this last vestige of form
disappeared and the consciousness itself was absorbed into
the Unutterable, the Ineffable.

The return towards the consciousness of the individual
body took place very slowly in a constant and invariable
splendour of Light and Power and Felicity and Adoration,
by successive gradations, but directly, without passing
again through the universal and terrestrial forms. And
it was as if the modest corporeal form had become the
direct and immediate vesture, without any intermediary,
of the supreme and eternal Witness.

This is a letter that the Mother sent to Sri Aurobindo and to which he answered on December 31, 1915:

> The experience you have described is Vedic in the real sense, though not one which would easily be recognised by the modern systems of Yoga which call themselves Vedic. It is the union of the "Earth" of the Veda and Purana with the divine Principle, an earth which is said to be above our earth, that is to say, the physical being and consciousness of which the world and the body are only images. But the modern Yogas hardly recognise the possibility of a material union with the Divine.

Why is this letter and Sri Aurobindo's response to it significant? First, it records an identification of the individual consciousness with the earth's consciousness, which is itself a remarkable experience. Then it describes the ascent of earth's consciousness towards the Divine and their eventual merging into one. Finally, it depicts the slow return of the new identification to the cosmic and then the individual consciousness with the fullest cognizance and attention to the microscopic details.

It also depicts how a spiritual experience may be symbolically described and experienced or how even the symbol may be an experience to a spiritual consciousness. The difference between her description and Sri Aurobindo's *Vishvaroop Darshana* seems to be that Sri Aurobindo's seems to be a witness throughout his realization, while the Mother embodied the experience as part of her being. This might be one of the differences between the Vedantic and Tantrik experiences that became so significant in post-Vedic developments of Indian spirituality.

It also confirms how great a spiritual being the Mother herself was and how Sri Aurobindo could comment on it with authority, confirming his own realizations about which he was usually silent. But what is this Vedic experience that Sri Aurobindo alludes to and how is it relevant today?

It is one of the traditions in Indic darshanas to recognize the great authority of the Veda and their acceptance as *Sruti*, the revealed scripture, recorded by the rishis of the Veda in the ancient texts. And the Veda is a stupendous repository of spiritual experience, though described in a symbolic language with terms in Vedic Sanskrit that are multidimensional and multi-layered. To appreciate them one needs to approach them with an awareness that is at once at the same level as that of the ancient rishis who were giants in yogic stature and accomplishments. Sri Aurobindo did this for us. For he was having these experiences on his own without an earlier grounding and training in Veda. And when he stumbled across the Veda it confirmed his own psychological movements that he had been unable to explain earlier in light of modern psychology or yogic descriptions. But he read in the Veda hints and representations of what he was himself undergoing. And he could appreciate their esoteric poetry and respond to it, as one seer to another.

Sri Aurobindo was able to unearth the ancient spiritual discoveries of the Veda that had subsequently been forgotten or misunderstood. And as Vedanta became more identified with *Mayavada*, itself misunderstood, its original impetus in the Veda became aligned with materialistic ritualism and *karmakanda*.

Sri Aurobindo showed us that the original *Srutis* were far more integral in vision and action than what the future developments understood them to be. That the Gita's embrace of action in Karma Yoga, even to the point of fighting as a hero in a universal war, was not a deviance from the Vedic line of the complete development of the individual and society. The Vedanta did not reject matter or the world to withdraw into an exclusive ivory tower or Himalayan cave, but matter itself was a manifestation of the Divine, as equally as mind. Or, as it has been said in later Buddhist literature, that the *samsara* is Nirvana and Nirvana is *samsara*.

The Veda went even deeper. It affirmed experientially that the highest consciousness or *Satyam-Ritam-Brihat* was present in the inconscience of matter. Or as it symbolically portrayed, the rays of Sun were trapped in the crypts of matter that were released by the Vedic rishis with the sound of mantra. Sri Aurobindo described the same when he stated in more modern terms that the Supramental consciousness is involved in the dense unconsciousness of matter and is evolving slowly and universally through life or the vital, through mind, and moving upward through higher planes of consciousness.

This hidden or buried consciousness in matter is alive and dynamic and can awaken, as it appears to be latent and asleep to our eyes and reality. For it can hold the minutest atom and the hugest galaxies together. So, is there a consciousness of the earth that is as supra-intelligent as the highest strata of divine awareness or *sat-chit-ananda*? The Veda accepts the hidden reality of earth-consciousness, and it is this that the Mother experienced in her personal identification with earth. And the Veda perceived that even matter and the earth could be transformed by releasing the hidden Sun in the rock through the *yajna* of self-surrender, *tapasya*, and the highest invocation of the Divine with the power of Yoga and mantra. The Mother confirmed this in the fact of her own *adhyatmik siddhi*, or yogic accomplishment.

Is such a transformation of earth possible? And can spirituality help us attain it? Is there a spiritual basis for such an aspiration? And if there is, what is the detailed pathway of Truth, the *ritasya panthah*, that can be followed to accomplish the same? The Veda says yes and shows us the pathway to immortality, individual and universal. Sri Aurobindo and the Mother showed us that the Vedic prayer for *amritam* or immortality was not vain but consistent with their highest attainments, and is a truth that the Vedic cycle awakens in us again.

Sri Aurobindo held that a divine life on earth is possible for mankind and spiritual transformation of all aspects of human life, not only envisionable but a distinct possibility and necessity for our future. It seems that this promise was present in seed in the Veda. If there is one master key to Veda, it is perhaps perfection. Veda aspires for humanity to reach perfection through the discovery of Truth, at all levels and *lokas*, by living in Unity and Bliss and offering all of oneself to the Divine Reality alone. Veda is a document of this deep aspiration of mankind and its promise of fulfillment.

The Experience of *Vala* Without the Symbolism

Her is another experience of the Mother that was narrated to Sat Prem, who compiled *Mother's Agenda* from November 8, 1958, which is almost reminiscent of the *Vala* myth, in her simple and direct language:

> I noticed that these children who had had a whole week to prepare their questions on the text had not found a single one! A terrible lethargy! A total lack of interest. And when I had finished speaking, I thought to myself, 'But what IS there in these people who are interested in nothing but their personal little affairs?' So I began descending into their mental atmosphere, in search of the little light, of that which responds ... And it literally pulled me downwards as into a hole, but in such a material way; my hand, which was on the arm of the chair, began slipping down, my other hand went like this (to the ground), my head, too! I thought it was going to touch my knees!
>
> And I had the impression ... It was not an impression—I saw it. I was descending into a crevasse between two steep rocks, rocks that appeared to be made of something harder than basalt, BLACK, but metallic at the same time, with such sharp edges—it seemed that a mere touch would lacerate you. It appeared endless and bottomless, and it kept getting narrower, narrower and narrower, narrower and narrower, like a funnel, so narrow that there was almost no more room—not even for the consciousness—to pass through. And the bottom was invisible, a black hole. And it went down, down, down, like that, without air, without light, except for a sort of glimmer that enabled me to make out the rock edges. They seemed to be cut so steeply, so sharply ...

Finally, when my head began touching my knees, I asked myself, 'But what is there at the bottom of this ... this hole?'

And as soon as I had uttered, 'What is there at the bottom of this hole?' I seemed to touch a spring that was in the very depths—a spring I didn't see but that acted instantly with a tremendous power—and it cast me up forthwith, hurled me out of this crevasse into ... (arms extended, motionless) a formless, limitless vast which was infinitely comfortable—not exactly warm, but it gave a feeling of ease and of an intimate warmth.

This is a clear direct description that gives us a perspective on the symbolic language of the Veda and what the rishis had attempted in their *yajna*. It seems that she had reached into *adri* and found the rays of light, the *Gau*, that were hidden in there.

To me, this experience, among many of the Mother, shows the continuity of Veda in her personal journey. It seems like she has opened this quintessentially Vedic experience to all humanity in a new and modern cycle of human evolution.

The Surya in *Adri*

Another experience of the Mother from Volume 2 of *Mother's Agenda*, Nov 7, 1961, is extremely significant here,

Then we descended into the Physical—and all the trouble began. But we didn't stay in the Physical, we descended into the Subconscient and from the Subconscient to the Inconscient. That was how we worked. And it was only when I descended into the Inconscient that I found the Divine Presence—there, in the midst of Darkness.

It wasn't the first time; when I was working with Theon at Tlemcen (the second time I was there), I descended into the total, unindividualized—that is, general—Inconscient (it was the time he wanted me to find the Mantra of Life).

And there I suddenly found myself in front of something like a vault or a grotto (of course, it was only something 'like' that), and when it opened, I saw a Being of iridescent light reclining with his head on his hand, fast asleep. All the light around him was iridescent. When I told Theon what I was seeing, he said it was 'the immanent God in the depths of the Inconscient,' who through his radiations was slowly waking the Inconscient to Consciousness.

But then a rather remarkable phenomenon occurred: when I looked at him, he woke up and opened his eyes, expressing the beginning of conscious, wakeful action.

I have experienced the descent into the Inconscient many times (you remember, once you were there the day it happened—it had to do with divine Love); this experience of descending to the very bottom of the Inconscient and finding there the Divine Consciousness, the Divine Presence, under one form or another. It has happened quite frequently.

This again, is the *Vala* symbolism given a more modern and direct language by another mystic of our times. When we review this further, the concept of the Supermind is akin to what is described as *Satyam-Ritam-Brihat* in the Veda. Or that of the Truth-Consciousness, which is a dynamic and integral unity of the highest awareness, named *as Rit-Chit* in the Veda. Sri Aurobindo states this clearly, therefore bringing a completion of cognition and fulfillment in the new age, bringing to a full circle the ancient prophecy and prayer of a universal awakening after an age of darkness, the *Kali Yuga*, by the Vedic rishis.

A new path has been opened up by Sri Aurobindo and the Mother. Or shall we rather say the old path has been cleared and made visible by these two great yogis in simultaneity and comradeship, to show us the possibilities that the future holds in the Vedic dawn coming back with the new strength and light of all the ancient dawns that have been there before.

9

The Vedic Way of Thinking

Is there a Vedic way of thinking? The answer is yes. It is a unified or synthetic way of perceiving, feeling, conceiving, and creating. It is not reductionistic or analytical but sees the hidden unity of all things, attempts to discover it, and adopt it in every manner of living. It is also synergistic and integral, assimilative, and absorptive. And it can live with apparent contradictions on the surface, holding the diverse poles together in a vast synthetic vision.

Then is there such a way of thinking that can be identified as the Indic way? For the Indic way on the surface often appears to be a panoply of confusing inter-mix of ideas, a medley of thoughts that look at the world differently and perhaps even contradict each other. For even in India there have been paths such as Jainism, Buddhism, or *Charvaka's* Materialism that reject the authority of the Veda. In my mind there is no significant disharmony between the Vedic Vedanta or Jainism. And Buddhism is Vedantic in approach and conclusion, even though it rejects Sanskrit as the language of communication and shuns Vedic ritualism while using the mythology, symbology, psychology, and insights of Veda and Vedanta.

And then what is this so-called religion called Hinduism that does not resemble traditional religions at all? It does not have one prophet, a set of unchanging beliefs or rituals, a single scripture, or any mandatory requirement. In fact, the word Hindu has come either from the Vedic word *Indu* (as noted earlier in chapter 3), which implies the land of Soma or the glow of moon or *Sindhu* which would hint at Sarasvati, the river of inspiration and light descending from above. If this is accepted, then the word Hindu might be more than a religious tag and may tie the Hindu at least linguistically to the Veda. And how does it relate to the term Sanatana Dharma, the Eternal Way of Being, which too has been not fully understood?

One characteristic that is immediately obvious even at a cursory glance is the all-embracing and all-encompassing attitude of the Vedic and Vedantic mind in all these terms. Diverse and seemingly contradictory impulses, practices, rituals, and belief-systems are assimilated and absorbed into a unique amalgam that can no longer be identified as a religion in the normal sense of the word. The term Hinduism has been abused lately by some zealots without understanding it fully. That the *Rig Veda* has influenced a large part of Sanatana Dharma and its various darshanas, and perhaps even the so called *Nastika* traditions.

The underlying theme of the Vedic way was a journey into the inner worlds and mastery over them. No other record of the time from any other part of the world describing such mysteries exists. And, most importantly, this inner journey, relentless and fearless, confirmed the underlying unity of the whole Universe in the strictest Monism ever articulated by mankind to this day. The term Absolute Monism is usually reserved for Advaita Vedanta, propagated by Adi Sankara. But Absolute Monism not only of the origin of things, but also their substance and essence, may be seen in all the *Srutis*. Perhaps a better term for this Monism is non-dualism, what the word *advaita* truly means.

So, the challenge of Sanatana Dharma is that it is not a religion, but we compare it with religions and try to fit it in the mold of being a theology. We may perhaps call it a way of seeing and being, as Sri Aurobindo said, "where the Many is One and the One is Many."

It is due to this non-dualism taken to its completest understanding that we see the whole plethora of completely contradictory and opposite philosophies being taken as valid in the practices that form the corpus of Sanatana Dharma. Each individual is free to create and live his own. In a sense, this is completely liberating. And yet, it puts the entire responsibility on the individual to take onus of his or her own understanding, development, refinement, and eventual direction. If this is understood, one can understand the confusion that one sees among many writers and thinkers of our times.

In his essay "Is There an Indian Way of Thinking? An Informal Essay," published in *Contributions to Indian Sociology* (1989), A.K. Ramanujan wondered if Indians "may be using a different logic" altogether. Some thinkers believe that such logic is an earlier stage of 'cultural evolution' and that Indians have not developed a notion of 'data,' of objective facts."

He quotes Sudhir Kakar, a psychoanalyst, who states,

> Generally among Indians, there seems to be a different relationship to outside reality, compared to the one met with in the West. In India, it is closer to a certain stage in childhood when outer objects did not have a separate, independent existence but were intimately related to the self and its affective states.... the world of magic and animistic thinking lie closer to the surface; so the grasp of reality is relatively tenuous.

There may be some truth to Ramanujan's and Kakar's observations. One only needs to look at the formulae of the Veda, such as *Tad Ekam* and *Satyam-Ritam-Brihat*, and the Upanishads' 'tat tvam asi' and 'so hum' to realize that the Indians generalize at the far deeper and unitary orders of existence than those of Western philosophers. There is none more unitary than the Indian when he says, 'riten ritam apihitam dhruvam,' or 'sarvam khalvidam brahma,' or 'etad vai tat.' The difficulty with the generalizations made by the Indians is that they go beyond intellectualism and speculation to psychological and experiential formulations that are not conceivable to the average human mind. And if the generalization is so general that it is applicable everywhere and anywhere, it tends to get overlooked in the practical world unless one is practicing intensely the spiritual disciplines of practical psychology called Yoga in India. Thus, it usually means nothing in *vyavhara*, to the practical man or to the intellectual, and is deemed to be nonexistent.

There are no external rules here, no moral or ethical dicta, edicts, or *farmaans*. And such a profound unitary rule paradoxically gives the utmost freedom and latitude to the individual. There is no abstract reality out there; it is all lived intensely, personally by the practicing seeker. Thus, all subsequent declarations that deal with more superficial matters become nuanced and seem applicable only to a particular situation or time-space, or to a particular kind of person.

The Indian paradigm belongs to another *anukrama*, or order of experience that underlies the Western approach to blanket universalisms without them being universal. This is almost akin to the Einsteinian world being another order to the model of the Newtonian world, or the paradigm of quantum mechanics that forms the substrate in the modern understanding of the Rutherfordian atomic model in physics.

Obviously, any such generalizations as mine about India itself would be flawed and self-contradictory, since Indians defy generalizations at least on the surface. If it is true that Indian culture even today is together because it springs from the artesian wells of Vedas and Vedanta then this too is easy to understand.

India confuses, confounds, and confronts with its myriad array, which is spiritual and materialistic, subtle, cultured, and gross, as discussed in chapter 3. Even time and space, the universal frames of reference, are inconstant. Rules change by *yugas* and *kula, jati* and *ritu. Ritu,* as Louis Renou points out, in *Sanskrit et*

Culture, is "not just a season, but also a crucial moment in Vedic sacrifice. There is a constant flowing together in *samsara* (which is the literal meaning of the word) and the body too is not just physical, it has also subtle and causal aspects."

The Vedic way of thinking is subtle, nuanced, fluid, wide, and open. Indians traditionally have thought a lot (and even argued a lot). The more qualified understanding of an Indian way of thinking at the highest level is that it is not only immensely refined but also one that comes after a long preparatory development in self-refinement. Unfortunately, this refinement was restricted to only a select few in Vedic times, perhaps due to the simple nature of the members of its society. And any attempt to spread the word had to use simplifications with its national epics, music, arts, darshanas, mythology, education, social and political sciences, and economic theory. This is where it began getting confusing. For, epics such as Mahabharata included multiple and diverse viewpoints of powerful personages in unique situations. Epics such as the Ramayana had almost 300 various tellings—each with its own storyline and interpretations, and the only common theme among all of them was perhaps the central place of the protagonists, Rama and Sita, and the tectonic shift in human society and evolution with their incarnation.

In some of these Ramayanas, even the narrative changes. What is fascinating is that the Indian mind presented its national hero and ideal from the multiple perspectives of different authors and poets. This was a very interesting co-creation across different micro-cultures of India and across various times and regions using the same symbols and characters, each with an interesting take and interpretations. Somehow the central event of Rama's life stayed in the national consciousness and transformed the culture and mind of the nation at a crucial juncture of its development. A profusion of creativity and diversity of opinion and approach is my impression on looking at this stupendous list of almost 300 different renderings. This may be a clue to the

Indian mind, which perplexes and impresses the modern mind greatly. We do not need to turn into zealots or fiery partisans and take sides in spiritual matters, and perhaps that is one of the lessons of India and the Veda. And it may be possible that those who claim to be the most Indian may become the least Indian if they do not understand the uniqueness of the Indian mind. This mind, in my opinion, was first seen in the Veda, and we continue to see it manifest itself in a panoply and splurge of visions and articulations. This original impetus of thought and its energies is perhaps still not lost in the confusion of modern India. For it is still latent and subterranean in my opinion and springs at the slightest opportunity and can always resurface when we question the meaning of India. This was first seen in the magnificent collective, shared profusion and outpouring of the Veda.

It seems to me that the Indian mind can be highly contextual but can also be context-free, and that is one of the aspects of its genius. We see in the Veda how this mind manifests. It is a mind that speaks in symbols, though the symbols are not restricted into metaphor but are freed up. For example, the symbol Agni is not restricted to a particular modality of worship, meaning, relationship, invocation, or praise of the gods. It has been liberated of all binding attachments. And like the French symbolist poet Stéphane Mallarmé, its associations to one subject have been removed, so that the symbol becomes independent and is able to form multiple relationships on its own. The symbol is made autonomous and independent of particular meaning.

Personally, I would hope that if India moves to a context-free way of thinking, it would be through the discovery of its own innate genius and the tremendous discoveries of its ancient past, although, necessarily, the modern formulation would be different. But it will need to be as wide and cosmopolitan as the Veda to have a lasting impact.

Modern physics has shown us that paradoxical states of being can co-exist, like the wave and particle theories of light there can be uncertainty in the very definition of sub-atomic particles, and we can have superposition and entanglement of these particles. This ability to hold opposing or contradictory thoughts at the same time is not necessarily a sign of immaturity or confusion but may indicate a more wholesome and synthetic mind.

Thus, the Vedic and Vedantic mind was able to question anything and everything radically, and was able to reject it all to start afresh perennially, *neti neti* (not this, not this). To never be satisfied or complacent, to experiment and explore boldly. For if there was ever an Indian way of thinking, it was this: not proceeding from fear but with innocence and profound questioning. And not rejecting one's own way of being, even if it meant rejecting the more successful and superficially enticing thinking models of the West. To articulate clearly and simply; calmly and directly. As J. Krishnamurti noted that the crucial difference between Indic thought and Western thought is that the Indic began with doubt while the Western began with belief. We see *neti neti* as an approach for the first time in world literature in the *Nasadiya Sookta*, and since then it has grown to become a powerful way to help clear the mind of all residue and prejudices and take it to a realm beyond concepts. Let us attempt to fathom this profound rejection of all hypotheses,

> Then existence was not nor non-existence, the mid-world was not nor the Ether nor what is beyond. What covered all? Where was it? in whose refuge? what was that ocean dense and deep?
>
> Death was not nor immortality nor the knowledge of day and night. That One lived without breath by his self-law, there was nothing else nor aught beyond it.
>
> In the beginning Darkness was hidden by darkness, all this was an ocean of inconscience. When universal

being was concealed by fragmentation, then by the greatness of its energy That One was born.

That moved at first as desire within, which was the primal seed of mind. The seers of Truth discovered the building of being in non-being by will in the heart and by the thought; their ray was extended horizontally; but what was there below, what was there above? There were Casters of the seed, there were Greatnesses; there was self-law below, there was Will above. (RV X.129.1-5, translated by Sri Aurobindo)

Not just *neti neti*, for the Vedic thought also is capable of *Iti Iti*, This and This. If we read the *Hiranyagarbha Sukta* it begins with an image of wholeness or completeness, i.e., the womb. In the womb, just as the fetus is completely protected, and is whole, the *Hiranyagarbha* or the Golden Womb of the Universe is a spiritual realization. Of the Universe being complete and whole and full of the glow of oneness and light, and out of this wholeness arises another wholeness, which is always complete. Perhaps this is the precursor to the famous shloka of the Upanishads:

Poornam adah poornam idam poornat poornam udachyate
Poornamasya poornamadaya poornameva vashishyate

That is Whole. This is Whole. The Whole arises out of the Whole. And as the Whole arises out of the Whole, what remains too is the Whole.

Perhaps there is no bigger question facing the nation today than what Indic/Vedic/Sanatana/Hindu mind or thought truly is, if it is not a religion, and how must it grow or be replaced by something greater, stronger, truer. How are each of these terms that frequently get lumped together variously nuanced and differentiated? And how does understanding Veda or thinking about it change Bharata, which literally means people deeply involved in discovering the Light and its manifestations, as discussed in chapter 3. This self-lit way, this thinking made luminous by the glow of the Self or *Atman*, may be the Indian way of thinking. This, its genius. And it may be recovered and re-discovered in modern life.

For *neti neti* is an approach that can lose all its traditions, *panthas*, literatures, philosophies, and yet recreate all fresh from nothing. The clue to its richness is that one can withdraw into the zero and create a Universe from it anew, alive. The Vedic Vedantic mind loves clean slates capable of revamping its *parampara* in every age. It is not afraid of nothing. Rather, it loves the Void and thrives on it. And this teaches us that we lose nothing and gain the world if we celebrate both *Nasti* (non-being) as well as *Asti* (being). We know that Brahman is both All and Nothing and yet always beyond. Established in this understanding we can fulfill the Vedic aspiration for the Victory of Truth.

The attempt to contextualize that which can eternally be free of all contexts and be the context itself is at the root of this ability to be free of all roots and yet be able to create an eternal journey that is autonomous, self-sustaining, and free of contradictions and limitations. Thus, the seeker can follow the Vedic *paramparas* with the deepest *bhava* and feeling, and yet be able to drop them as he or she climbs upward in consciousness and truth-realization. And this ability to leave everything, walk away, and yet be complete and whole is perhaps what may be the Indic way of thinking, right from the Veda to our times.

Why is this relevant? It is important to experiment with this 'negative thinking,' as J. Krishnamurti used to call it. Or the 'mind eternally empty,' as Sri Aurobindo used to describe his own mental state. For in this void is the Supreme Possibility of creation, joy, and discovery.

Some of these confusions about the place of India in the community of nations arise because the original geniuses, brought out in the Veda, which has been forgotten. If we had the true interpretation of its hymns available to us, then issues such as contextualization would not arise. If contextualization is indeed required, then it may need to have the Vedic Vedantic background. And if one is capable or willing to discard everything, even the Veda, then it can be only on a spiritual basis that encompasses all diversities in its Oneness, again on lines that are Vedic in essence.

The Vedic way of thinking can afford to drop all premises and postulates and resume entirely from nothing, as noted. It can have the ground underneath pulled away and yet be able to build the cosmos, as we see in the *Nasadiya Sutra*. In fact, this thought revels in the tabula rasa, to reject everything and start from ground zero.

The Veda is thus like the cosmic microwave background of modern physics, the uniform distribution of radiation that is present with us always since it was released at the time of the Big Bang. And it is also the Big Shebang of our literary, intellectual, and artistic Universe. It paradoxically reminds me of the postmodern world "where the concept of truth is subject to many differing variations and interpretations," as Deirdre Bair pointed out in her book *Jung*. The Veda shows us that we may have One Truth and Infinite Truths simultaneously, that they are not incompatible, and each of them is valid and relevant in its time and space, poise, and state.

So, if we wish to understand the Indian way of thinking, we may need to re-discover its genius. And perhaps re-visit the Veda and Vedanta in their integrality, not from a narrow perspective. And appreciate with empathy what the rishis were trying to tell us and with what consciousness. For if we can even begin to glimpse their awareness and thought, we will begin to grow. If we can understand what they understood and experienced as their model of the Universe, our consciousness will change radically. But for that great dedication and sincerity is needed, along with openness and sensitivity. For the Veda is a way of feeling and being and connecting the *Sruti* that can be seen even today by those eyes that are willing to behold without their own screens.

We need to develop a subtlety of thought and wideness of perspective. And as thought grows finer and more elevated, it can rise to higher reaches of consciousness. The Veda did not reject thinking. But it always attempted to raise the mental consciousness to higher planes, 'climbing Indra like a ladder,' in the words of Veda. This sublimity of thought would reveal greater splendors beyond thought until it reached its highest origin and inspiration.

As Sri Aurobindo sings in his poem "Thought the Paraclete":

As some bright archangel in vision flies …
Flew my thought self-lost in the vasts of God.
Sleepless wide great glimmering wings of wind
Bore the gold-red seeking of feet that trod…
Over world-bare summits of timeless being…
Sun-realms of supernal seeing…

Thought the great-winged wanderer paraclete
Disappeared slow-singing a flame-word rune.
Self was left, lone, limitless, nude, immune.

10

Sri Aurobindo's Darshana and Its Correspondence with the Veda

Let us now briefly review how Sri Aurobindo's darshana has its correspondences or parallels with the Vedic model of the Universe. When we study his 'philosophy,' we may often find it complex and difficult, but perhaps it can become easier by seeing the Vedanta in Sri Aurobindo's worldview and darshana.

Simply put, Sri Aurobindo's darshana confirms the fundamental unity of the Universe. This unitary principle is called the Brahman, not seizable by mind, but present and real to the luminous and intuitive states of human consciousness. This Brahman is omnipresent, omniscient, and omnipotent. It is transcendental as well as immanent, cosmic as well as individual. It is beyond words since it is the state of Oneness, and that is why it is called *anirvacaniya* (that which cannot be spoken about) and *anirdeshiya* (that which has no direction).

Brahman manifests itself in form as various worlds or *lokas*. The highest *loka* known to man's awareness is that of *sat-chit-ananda*, truth-consciousness-bliss, which is the highest manifestation of Brahman. *Sat-chit-ananda* manifests the worlds of matter, life, and mind via the principle or agency of the Supermind, which is truth-consciousness or *rit-chit* in the Veda.

The upper half or *Parardha* thus comprises *sat, chit,* and *ananda*, which is separated from the lower half or *Aparardha* with the intermediate *loka* of the Supermind. The three *lokas* beneath the Supermind are *Manas* or mind, *Prana* or the vital and *Annam* or matter. Brahman is equally present in Supermind as it is in matter, although it is veiled in the latter (when the Veda talks about the Sunrays or *Gau* hidden in the crypts or *bila* of *adri* or matter, it is symbolically saying the same thing).

Sri Aurobindo also described the Psychic Being, which is the Divine Brahman present in the center of each individual's psycho-physical body and is the consistent thread through its various births. This psychic being too is eternal, pure, and can never be hurt or destroyed, *anahata*. And it is the principle of Brahman involved in matter that is its secret aspiration to ascend again to the Supermind and above. This psychic being is described in the Veda as Agni or Divine Love.

Sri Aurobindo is a unique synthesis of higher Tantra and Vedanta who embraces all manifestations of reality. His Yoga is an integral Yoga, in that all life becomes a means to an ascent in knowledge and light towards a realization of higher truths and Divine existence. His insight into evolution too is Vedic in that the Supermind is involved in the Nescient and all of evolution is but an unfolding of the secret Supermind from the Subconscious and the Inconscient.

This, in short, is a very limited summary of the darshana of Sri Aurobindo. Of course, there is much more, to elaborate which he had to write more than 37 volumes of encyclopedic works. The Veda too is vast and seemingly complex, but its underlying schema is simple and clear. The attempt to show the correspondence between Sri Aurobindo and the Veda is not only to study the Veda in the light of Sri Aurobindo's spiritual realizations but also to make them easier to approach or grasp by the human mind.

If we understand either or both, we can understand Sri Aurobindo's explanation of Evolution and Integral Yoga, which are Vedic in approach and elaboration; integral Vedanta as contrasted with the *Mayavadi* Vedanta becomes clear. So do Tantra, Bhakti Yoga, Karma Yoga, Sankhya, and Buddhism among other Indian *panthas*, as we understand the roots they come from. Sri Aurobindo thus represents the best of

non-sectarian Sanatana Dharma. It is important to see him as
continuing with the Vedic way and not departing from it. The
most important feature Sri Aurobindo and the Vedic darshana
share is this integrality of vision, all-inclusiveness and desire for
the human ascent and divine perfection.

A Schema of Correspondences Between Sri Aurobindo and the Veda

The spiritual psychological paradigm of the Veda in the modern
language of Sri Aurobindo:

Vedic	Vedic Symbol/ Deva	Sri Aurobindo's Terminology
Tad Ekam, Tad Satyam	Hiranyagarbha, Prajapati	That One, The Brahman
Satyam-Ritam-Brihat, Rit-Chit	Soorya	Supermind, Truth-Consciousness
	Indra	Luminous Mind
Prana	*Vayu/Ashvins*	The Vital
	Adri	Matter, Hill of being
	Salilam Apraketam	The Inconscient
Chaitya Purusha	Agni	The Psychic

IV

Yajna and the Fourfold Godhead of the Veda

11

The Symbol as Meditation

The Veda, as we have seen, may be considered as the earliest manual for *dhyana* or meditation and we have discussed some of its methods in chapter 5. These techniques later bloomed into various Indic schools of Yoga, Tantra, Sankhya, and Bhakti, with their highly developed and specialized methods that are widely in use even today. However, as discussed, the language of Veda is symbolic, archetypal, and veiled from the surface eye. But if we consider its clues attentively, we may discern how our present insights into meditation may have taken root in its early divinations.

We may suggest here that each symbol in Veda is meditation. That is, it is not only a sign of something else, it is also an esoteric reality that can reach deep in one's consciousness and influence it radically. It is here that Vedic symbology exceeds modern linguistic and semiotic analyses, where the symbol is just an intellectual concept.

For instance, if we begin to see Agni as the Divine Love within us, our *Purusha* or Pure Consciousness, then right from the first Sukta we enter a mystical domain of sacred and hieratic experience.

The first mantra of Veda invokes Agni thus,

I adore the Flame, the vicar, the divine Ritwik of the yajna, the summoner who most founds the ecstasy.

Agni as our *Hrdi Purusha*, the Consciousness seated in the heart, is no longer a physical fire, but an intimate experience that is invoked and expanded. When the rishi calls Agni the compass and the grace and light encompassing from all sides in the spiritual journey, or as the eminent leader, this is not poetic fancy for those who can share its original inspiration and feeling.

Or when Agni is called the Poet or the Seer-Will, that too suddenly turns it from an objective reality to something keenly felt and lived. An inner eye suddenly opens to the domain of the rishi. This is not an external fire but our innermost reality.

What are the others clues to reach the Truth according to the Veda? Invoke the Agni and offer it *Ghritam*! *Ghritam* is not just purified butter but a luminous clear dense mind. When such a state is offered to the Divine within, there is rapid growth in the blaze of the fire in *yajna* (more on this in the next chapter on Agni).

Once Agni is invoked and intensified, Soma is produced, which is offered to Indra and Vayu. What does this mean? The *tejas* of Agni changes the body's physiology and psychology, which generates bliss. That bliss transforms mind and *prana*. Veda uses a symbolic language to describe the yogic experience of how the mind and vitality are metamorphosed in the first realization of bliss by the seeker.

How to hold bliss in the consciousness or Soma in the *kalasha*, or container of the heart? First, discover the bliss that is always hidden within oneself. Be still and perceive. Second, grow in self-purification and intensify concentration (grow Agni). Third, learn to hold without distraction or dissipation, in *dharana,* with utmost patience, without preference.

Myth as Meditation

As suggested earlier, even myths are symbols in Veda. We discussed the myths of *Vritra* and *Vala* earlier and how they signify spiritual secrets that were elucidated by Sri Aurobindo and the Mother through their own commentaries and experiences. The myth of

Agni and its return to the *yajna* is another profound symbol in the Veda (*Rig Veda* X.51-54). Agni hides in the waters because his elder brothers who had carried the offering to the Devas have died. Yama and Varuna find him and grant him immortality so that he may return to the *yajna*. Here, Yama is the guardian of *dharma*, and self-mastery, and in later developments, the deva of death. Varuna is the deva of wideness in the emotional mind and a vast purity. The hidden powers of Agni are discovered by them and brought to the *yajna* as a deva who is immortal among the mortals, *martyeshu amritah*. Agni rises from the latency of waters and dormancy among the growths of earth to become the dynamic principle of yogic *tapasya* in *yajna*. This is the secret of Agni, the Divine in our hearts who is eternal and imperishable, *ajaram*.

Or when we consider the myth of *Shunahshepa* (*Rig Veda* I.24.1-15), who is to be sacrificed at the *yajna*, after his father sells him to be *purusha-pashu*, the human sacrifice, but the rishis refuse to participate in the ceremony. *Shunahshepa*, which literally means the tail of a dog implying the fixity of personality or habit, prays to Varuna to free him. Varuna, the wideness of emotional mind, liberates him from the three cords of bondage that hold him, the physical, *pranic*, and mental, and *Shunahshepa* is accepted into the fraternity of the rishis. Vishvamitra, the famous rishi, adopts him and calls him *Devavrata*, someone who has kept his vow to the devas. This description by rishi *Shunahshepa* of his own life couches the spiritual journey of freedom from his constrictions through the agency of Varuna, the deva of expansiveness and emotional maturity due to that widening.

The myth of Angirasa rishis is another powerful message in the Veda. They were the earliest rishis who ascended to a station above that of the devas and who assist the devas in *yajna*. They are also said to be the first offsprings of Agni and the roots of their names *anga-* is brilliantly suggestive of this fundamental relationship and their closeness with Agni. But their myth also brings home to the aspirant the immense potential of each human being and his or her capacity to ascend higher than the devas. Such depiction of radical human possibilities makes the Veda a unique document among all world scriptures and literature.

Additionally, not only are these myths parables and living symbols, but they are also the fulfillment of possibilities, making this achievement easier to accomplish for generations to come. The legend of *Kutsa* travelling with Indra in a chariot until he becomes exactly like Indra, so much so that only Sachi, Indra's wife, can tell them apart, is a spiritual fable of the human and the divine in camaraderie and journey together. As Sri Aurobindo elaborates in *The Doctrine of the Mystics*,

> (Rishis such as) Kanwa, Kutsa, Atri, Kakshiwan, Gotama, Shunahshepa have become types of certain spiritual victories which tend to be constantly repeated in the experience of humanity. The seven sages, the Angirasas, are waiting still and always, ready to chant the word, to rend the cavern, to find the lost herds, to recover the hidden Sun.

Vedic Numerology, Morphology, and Semantics

Even numbers are of symbolic significance in Veda. For example, the number three when mentioned implies our existence on earth in body, life, and mind. Or it may refer to the unity of *satyam-ritam-brihat*. Or say, the number seven, which usually implies the seven *lokas* or worlds of our simultaneous existence.

Tatyana Elizarenkova in the *Language and Style of Rsis* has shown how the structure or morphology of the Vedic hymns are structured to aid meditation. For instance, in *Rig Veda* Sukta III.20, "Each stanza (except the last one) begins with the god's (Agni's) name.... stanza 1a—*agnim*...; 2a—*agne*....; 3a—

agne....; 4a—*agnir....*; 5a—*agnim....*" She notes the 'figurative' level of Vedic hymns that have a 'programmatic character.' She seems to mean by this that the mantras not only have their own resonance of sound and significance, but also their organization into *suktas* and mandalas that have a profound suggestiveness and meditative quality. And she states that "the use of this hyper-semantization of the text is of exceptional importance for the whole hymnic collection."

Other uses of the structure of hymns to enhance their suggestiveness and allusions is described in detail by Joel P. Brereton and Stephanie W. Jamison in *The Rigveda: A Guide.* Even literary devices and *shlesha* or puns create another level of communication beyond the purely verbal.

Morphology is the study of the shape of the part and its relationship with other parts and with the whole, according to Vladimir Propp in *Morphology of the Folktale.* If we look at the whole selection and organization of Veda, there is a method behind the placements and structure. For example, if we compare the Creation Hymns, we will see a recurrence of imagery, and a movement of mind to that primal moment when one exists in a state of all possibility, beyond concepts and ideas. The contemplation of the Beginning of the Cosmos becomes a revelation about the nature of one's own mind and its return to one's primeval origins. Or how each *rik* relates to the other mantras in a *sukta*, or how the *suktas* relate to each other and the recurrence of the name of a particular deva in the *riks* of a *sukta* through root sounds. For example, in *Agni Suktam*, the use of sounds *anga-* and *angirasa* not only reinforce the various forms of Agni but also turn the etymology itself into a means of communication.

Semantics is the study of meaning. The Veda seems to move into a space beyond meaning into experience via the modalities of sound, myth, imagery, numerology, linguistics, and the structure and organization of the mantras. It turns texts, images, music, structure, and figures of speech into symbols of *dhyana.* And

those of us who have any experience with meditation realize that
one of the first steps is to drop the linear movement of thought
into realms where things happen together and simultaneously at
the level beyond sense and meaning.

Veda and the New Physics

As discussed in chapter 5 even time and space are transformed
in Veda. Time is not linear but cyclic as we see in the annual,
monthly, and daily cycles of *yajna*, *Usha*, Soma, and Surya. Time
is also *Kaala*, or the seed placed at the origin of the Universe
in the inconscient, that evolves according to its self-nature and
unfolds what it holds as germ. Time is also simultaneity of
multiple *lokas* in the central motif of the *yajna* that can make
creation happen with the power of mantra. Time itself is created
in the Creation Hymns by that which is beyond Time, and this
Timelessness can be reached by the seer with the power of *yajna*.

Space is not one but many. Briefly, it is *antariksha*, the
expanse of life-energy and *dyaus*, or the space of mind. It is
Parama Vyoma or Ultimate Sky, where consciousness beholds
the birth of mantra. What is accomplished in the *Parama Vyoma*
gets translated to the lower three *lokas* of mind, life, and matter,
showing the correspondence among the seven worlds. Thus, space
is not just physical but a multi-dimensional entity, no longer
confined to the three dimensions of gross senses. But it is capable
of infinite condensation, expansion, and concentration into the
bindu or point, becoming multi-layered with several horizons or
kshitija, and can close upon itself as in the *Hiranyagarbha*, or the
Golden Womb. It is unitary as in *Svara*, or the realm of Surya
above, and is also coiled in and buried as in the dense rock of
unconsciousness or *adri*.

The Veda makes available to us an endless meditation
of symbols that are visual, auditory, tactile, conceptual,
and ritualistic. And each symbol transcends itself into the

Undefinable, the Unknown Mystery, *Tad Adbhutam*. It may be sometimes instructive to study the Vedic frame of references with those of newer sciences such as Modern Physics.

For example, when Carlo Rovelli in his book *Helgoland* discusses the emptiness of each subatomic particle, he seems to imply something similar—that each so-called particle is defined only by its relationship to other particles. There is no fundamental substance that makes these particles. They have no original essence according to him.

In this vein, Rovelli also compares the model of subatomic physics with the *Shoonyavada* of Nagarjuna. According to Nagarjuna who lived in the 2nd century CE, all experienced phenomena are *shoonya* and have no value by themselves. Each entity is defined by its relationships to all the other entities. As one goes to the essence of each entity, all one finds is emptiness. The parallels between Quantum Physics and *Shoonyavada* are interesting. It may be pertinent to note here that each sub-atomic particle itself is only a concept or an image in our heads, a symbol too, as part of the paradigm provided by the Copenhagen Interpretation of Quantum Physics.

But the emptiness of *shoonya* is not a physical void. For it is beyond concept or ideation. It is neither empty nor full, neither truth nor untruth, neither *sat* nor *asat*. As we meditate on the *shoonya*, it takes us into another realm beyond words or ideations and transforms our awareness. Shoonya is not empty; it is our self-nature.

As I meditate on the implications of Rovelli's approach to Quantum Physics, it seems to me that the Veda itself is a beautiful symbol of this self-transcendence. Each deva and symbol dissolves and resolves into an Ultimate Unity, *Tad Ekam*, that is beyond any conceptualization possible to us, and that can only be experienced and lived. The *Tad Ekam* is Indescribable, *anirvacaniya*. I have always felt that the first articulation of this *shoonya* appears in the *Nasadiya Sukta*. And the first sophisticated paradigm of the symbol becoming multi-dimensional and capable of self-transformation in any literature happened in the Veda.

Each deva exists in a complex and dynamic interdependence with the other devas, never in isolation, and within the fundamental Unity that is Inconceivable to our mind. As Nagarjuna would say, they have no 'autonomous existence' or permanent, eternal substance, *svabhava*. All the key devas together create a composite, a whole. Remove one and the whole paradigm collapses. They arise as co-dependent beings.

We may justifiably say here that the Veda has used the symbol to its maximum possibility, effect, and transcendence in a comprehensive manner. The only literature that takes a similar approach is that of the symbolists in modern literature, but their range is much narrower, and their reach limited.

Veda and Jungian Psychology

Carl Gustav Jung in *Memories, Dreams, Reflections* discusses some concepts that share parallels with the Veda in their paradigm. His concept of the Collective Unconscious gives us an insight into the descriptions of *Salilam Apraketam* in the Veda, the sea of inconscience that underlies all of creation. Except that the Inconscient of Veda is even more dense and unconscious than the Collective Unconscious of Jung.

It is also curious how psychological and physical movements come together simultaneously in Jung's descriptions, what he called synchronicity. He says that there is an overlap between the inner and the outer, which is acausal and random but is common enough to tell us that there is some kind of connection beyond space and time. It appears that the Vedic model of the Universe with its seven *lokas* intermingling with each other, influencing each other and forming a single Unity in their essence of *Tad Ekam*, might be able to explain this phenomenon of synchronicity.

Joseph Campbell in *The Power of Myth* stated that the myth is our collective dream. But it seems to me that the myths of Veda, including those of *Vritra, Vala,* Agni, *Angirasa, Shunashepa,* the Creation hymns, among others, also represent unique human experiences as described in the field of hierology, or the dimension of the sacred. And the specialized human development, termed spiritual transformation or Yoga, is obvious in these tales. Similarly, Alchemy, the science of radical metamorphosis of oneself, another ancient human aspiration and myth studied extensively and elaborated by Jung, is a constant theme in Veda.

We have already discussed how the symbol or devas in Veda may represent universal archetypal images that are found across indigenous cultures in their art, folklore, mythology, and motifs. These images may seem dream-like but are not haphazard and have an inner consistency and reason. David Johnston in *Prophets in Our Midst* shows the overlaps between the visions of Sri Aurobindo and Jung. For example, the concept of the Self in Jung seems to parallel the principle of the Psychic Being in Sri Aurobindo.

The concept of individuation in Jung's psychology is another achievement similar to the principles of self-evolution in Vedic framework. The shadow is an insight into the nature and challenges of human existence like the Vedic concept of the *Dasyus* or the dark forces of the Universe (discussed in chapter 13).

Jung's Gnostic Creation Story of *Seven Sermons to the Dead* describes the origin of the Universe as the Pleroma, which is 'both emptiness and fullness, differentiated and undifferentiated, containing all the opposites in a state of equilibrium.' This description seems akin to the ancient Vedic hymns of creation where the source and birth is non-conceptual and unified.

There are many more overlaps between the paradigms of Veda and modern psychology, especially those of C.G. Jung and

Abraham Maslow. While they may not be taken literally, they give us a valuable reminder that Vedic psychology, symbolism, and mythology are every bit as sophisticated as modern thought, and sometimes exceed it in audacity and reach.

Subhash Kak in *The Gods Within* proposes that

> within the Indian tradition the gods are first and foremost the constituents of the individual's consciousness, and only secondarily the outer processes. They may be seen as the precognitive and cognitive centers in the brain or the archetypal projections of an objective consciousness on the subjective mind.

Perhaps these centers are akin to what are called chakras in traditional Yoga and Tantra as in ancient depictions of the psycho-physical body. Or they may correlate with the gross, subtle, and causal bodies as discussed in chapter 3.

In "A Three-Layered Model for Consciousness States," a paper by Arushi Kak, Abhinav Gautam, and Subhash Kak, "A three-level framework to represent different states of consciousness is proposed…The uncoupling of perception from sensory inputs supports the idea of a disembodied state. A consciousness state that is decoupled from specific memories of the individual indicates that such states have an ontological reality." I believe a new model of psychology is needed that can help study awareness rigorously and bring us up to speed with the ancient discoveries of Vedic rishis, who were no less scientific than modern researchers in their investigations.

The Medium of Veda

Marshall McLuhan famously said that the medium is the message, in his book with the same title, *The Medium is the Message: An Inventory of Effects*. The Veda is a unique medium or rather multi-medium that creates its own cognitive shifts. What prevents the Veda from turning into cliché is its range, depth, height, style, and complexity of interweaving threads that create new interpretations and ambiguities due to the nature of the text. Perhaps the future of humanity is *The Global Village* as imagined by McLuhan, but if so, it will need to assimilate the invocations for universal harmony and community that the Veda first articulated and aspired for.

The Veda is humanity's first "multi-media experience," according to Stephanie W. Jamison and Joel P. Brereton in *The Rigveda: The Earliest Religious Poetry of India*. This multi-media and multi-sensory experience involves almost all the senses including hearing, sight, smell, taste, and touch through the ritual and its ultimate transcendence. Not only does the Veda constantly engage and then reach beyond the senses, its images and meanings are fused together and take us to a synthetic way of thinking rather than the dualistic or analytic thought of the modern mind.

This is one of the earliest realizations of any meditation; that the mind itself is not the final arbiter and is itself extremely limited in its ability to analyze its data and make sense of the world or cope with it. Every movement, form, entity, sound, relationship, music, arrangement, literary device, linguistics, morphology, semiotics, etymology, and metaphysics may become a symbol in Veda due to its intentional design and worthy of intense and deep thinking. The moment we realize this, the Veda becomes sacred once again, filling us with the same wonder and awe that our ancient forefathers felt when they first beheld this world and its profusion of natural elements, forms, and forces.

12

Agni: The Divine Within

The true Veda is not a book out there. It is the inner knowing that we all have spontaneously. Thus, any reading of the Veda can only be a journey within, with the external text as a tool and a guide but not as replacement for our own exploration and discoveries. The outer *Sruti* is a grand and orchestral work, capturing echoes of our inner life in a performative, resonant art, of symbols and myths, a reminder of what we hold within ourselves eternally. But it comes to fruition only when we live it intensely and truly make it a part of our being.

Agni is an experience, not an imagination. It is awareness filled with glow. Anyone with the slightest experience of *dhyana* or meditation can relate to this inner light and flame. If this symbol that is an experience becomes alive to the seeker, each *rik* of Veda acquires a unique and nuanced significance. That is the state of mind one should be in when delving into the Veda.

Agni is the revelation of our own Truth to ourselves that appears to the subtle senses as Light and Fire. At higher levels of consciousness, it becomes *Jyoti*, or the Divine Light. It can also be seen as *Ojas*, the energy of Creation. It is also *Aabhaa* or glow of self-awareness and concentration. As physical fire, it gives *prakasa* or light.

With this understanding, let us proceed to study one of the most important devas and symbols of the third dimension of Veda, i.e., the spiritual. And try to experience Agni rather than just treating him intellectually. Studying Agni with the other three devas—Indra, Surya, and Soma—with the central oblation of the *yajna*, gives us another perspective on the magnificent tapestry of Veda with its complex designs, wefts, and woofs. It may also help us develop a different appreciation of these devas and their relationships. We begin with the first image, the primal *hieros*, i.e., Fire, called Agni in ancient Sanskrit—yet ubiquitous to us even in this technological age. The first verse of the *Rig Veda* invokes Agni as the priest, the *purohit*, the mediator, whom the seeker adores and honors.

अग्निमीळे पुरोहितं यज्ञस्य देवमृत्विजम् ।
होतारं रत्नधातमम् ॥ १ ॥

The Fire I pray, the divine vicar of the sacrifice and ordinant of the rite, the Summoner (or, priest of the offering) who most founds the ecstasy. (This is one of the early translations offered by Sri Aurobindo.)

The Roots of Agni

In a detailed etymological analysis of the word Agni, Sri Aurobindo showed in *Hymns to the Mystic Fire* that it comprises three root sounds, *a*, *ga*, and *na*, each with its own sound and psychological significance. The sound *a* signifies the beginning and absolute existence or 'to be.' *G-* is the Sanskrit root that indicates light and idea of force. "*Ag-* therefore means to exist in force, pre-eminently—to be splendid, strong, excellent and Agni means mighty, supreme, splendid, forceful, bright. We find the same root in the Greek *agathos* … meaning originally, strong, noble, brave; *ago*, I lead; *aglaos*, bright." And *n-* signifies movement or to lead. "It seems also to have meant to love, from the idea of embracing *ang*… (also it has) the sense of fire, *angarah*, a live coal," as Sri Aurobindo showed.

Linguistically, the word Agni shares its historical Sanskrit roots with other classical languages. For example, when we use words like Agnes, igneous, or ignite, which have a Latin base. Or the Greek *Agape*, which is still used today to describe various states or levels of love (compared to *Eros, Philia, Mania*, etc.). We are still deploying the same cognate sounds in our languages that have supposedly come to us from their Proto-Indo-European ancestor.

Sri Aurobindo adds, "Agni is the master of *tejas*, especially fiery *tejas*…in the language of modern psychology, … (Agni is) Will in action. Agni is purely mental force, necessary to all concentration."

Swami Dayananda in his *Rig Veda Bhasha Bhashya* showed that Agni derives from Sanskrit root *Agre-*, which implies the forefront of all our actions. David Frawley in *Wisdom of the Ancient Seers* calls him the inner guide (*agre netar*, leader in the front) and the indestructible *a-gni*, and the power of transformation.

The Physical, Emotional, Poetic Agni

Let us first look at Agni solely as Fire, the physical and chemical reaction. One of the earliest and most important discoveries of mankind that essentially transformed human civilization was the taming of fire about one million years ago. This was the beginning of human societies becoming safer, healthier, more comfortable, and in control of their destiny.

If we look at it as symbol, which it must have been to the Neolithic man, a mysterious and magical appearance, that he could yet control, we see how it must have shaped our collective psyche. And if we accept Jung's principle of archetypes, it seems to me that fire must have been one of the earliest experiences of man that gave him power, delight, and a new way to apprehend the elements and resources. Fire, thus, is a beautiful myth and we see this in the Greek story of Prometheus who stole it from the gods and was condemned to eternal punishment for bringing something to man that made him their equal.

As a poetic image, it is full of possibilities. As Percy Bysshe Shelley sang in *The Witch of Atlas*,

Men scarcely know how beautiful fire is—
Each flame of it is as a precious stone
Dissolved in ever-moving light, and this
Belongs to each and all who gaze upon.

Wallace Stevens invoked it in *The Owl in the Sarcophagus*, "A diamond jubilance beyond the fire." Sri Aurobindo sang of Agni in his lyric *Bride of the Fire*, with a rhythm reminding us of the subtle and delicate yet intense flame burning in our hearts,

Bride of the Fire, clasp me now close—
Bride of the Fire!
I have shed the bloom of the earthly rose,
I have slain desire.

Agni is thus, the first among devas and his hymns are among the most common in the Veda along with those on Indra; for he is the most accessible to humans and the most helpful.

If we look closely, we realize that Agni is not a thing or substance but a process and a principle of great beauty. It flows through our hectic and turbulent lives unseen in various streams, obvious or hidden. Even in matter as energy, in our homes or factories, in electric bulbs or in campfires, in our smart phones or kitchens, it is still as ubiquitous as it was a million years ago. Fire is our life and as we transform it, it transforms us.

Agni in Other Denominations

And yet, there are other manifestations of fire, for fire is not just a burning flame but is inextricably linked in Veda with light, brilliance, and energy. If we look at Agni, we might discern the flame of an eye, which suggests the ancient Indian phrase, "we do not see the light, but all is seen by the Light." I believe that this symbol of Invisible Light and Fire is the same as what appears in esoteric Christianity. In Sufism it is "the light beyond the light, *Nooren a la Noor.*" In Zoroastrianism, Agni represents God's light and wisdom. The burning bush too is an ancient symbol of this light brought to us by the ancient Judaic testament, as David Frawley has pointed out.

Light is equated with the Divine on the physical plane. An experience of its lucency and mystique in dreams, subconscious imagery and surreal art is usually a hint of grace, protection, strength, and positivity. Agni then is Divine Presence, Divine Grace, and the hidden spark or flame that energizes our life.

Physiological Agni

There is yet another manifestation of fire and that is in our physiology. It is the Life Force, the energy, the fever of life, the protoplasmic spark in the cell. It is the digestive fire in our stomach, *jathar agni*, and the fire of anger, *krodha agni*, and the fire of passion and desire, *kama agni*. In Vedic symbolism it is buried in the waters, and in the woods, and in the rocks as if inverted upon itself, cloaked in the dense darkness of its own choosing.

Finally, it is the effulgence and the radiance that always accompanies us as our core awareness, that is always with us whether we notice it or not, even physically. To our psyche, Agni is not just an image or the sixth element, but a powerful symbol and experience and the mind and heart's innate reality.

I have waxed eloquent about Agni and its various dimensions, because I wanted to show that it is not just a physical or material process. Even in our modern age, it retains its mystical nature that holds within it both fear and security, injury and warmth, beauty, and death. To our ancient ancestors living in a certain part of the Indian subcontinent several thousand years ago, it was no less a principle of great value and importance, rather significantly more so.

For the ancient mind of our ancestors was not yet intellectualized like ours. But it was simple, direct, free of the clutter and baggage that our modern minds are filled with, entranced with miraculous phenomena (and perhaps to them things were far more magical and fascinating than to us), absorbed more easily into what it beheld and able to feel more intensely with empathy and connectedness. It was not a mind we have today. And we can study the Veda to peer into the inner life of our forefathers. To me, the Veda is even more important than the Cuneiform script or the recent discovery of *Gobekli Tepe* in Turkey, which has upended all our fixed ideas about the Neolithic period. For the Veda is not just an archeological site, it is also alive in a language that is yet spoken, written, and used, and it is the seed that created the psychological-spiritual gestalt that we call today the Indic civilization.

It is critical then that we understand that to rishis of the Vedic age, Agni was the Divine itself. It was, to them, our purest element, the golden-white 'jubilance,' luminous, and revelatory, an inner realization and the enlightenment of human consciousness. For Agni is a process of intensification, purification, energization, concentration, aspiration, and self-realization. As Sri Aurobindo said in one of his letters, "Agni is the psychic fire.... When it burns in the heart.... The psychic fire is individual and takes usually the form of a fire of aspiration or personal Tapasya. This Fire is (also) universal and it (comes) from above."

Agni in the Veda

Agni is the principle that connects us to the Universe, and to the Divine elements that are latent in us. It is what leads us to the truth and the symbol that transcends the individual. Seated in our hearts, as our greatest sacredness, it is the divine flame that transcends us even as it is immanent. It is what gives us beauty, divinity, seerhood, willpower, knowledge, poetic capacity, and the ability to communicate with all other forces in the Universe, and is life itself. It is our first principle, the connector, which joins us with the Dawn and Indra with his thunderbolt and the Sun as the unifying power and creator of the Universe. And each of these, Dawn, Indra, and Sun too are Vedic symbols of profound significance if we can understand what Agni meant to the Vedic seers.

The symbolism of Agni runs through Indian cultures in various manifestations down to the modern times. And as we discussed, it flows down all human cultures and religions in various forms to this date. It is called various names such as *vaisvanara* (the universal being or man), *tanunapat* (he who births his body), *saptajihva* (the one with seven tongues, another multi-dimensional image implying the seven *lokas* as its home), *vishvavedasam* (one who is all-knowing), among others. Each name has a meaning that is obvious to one who approaches its symbol with openness, rapt with its eternal revelation. It represents all the gods and psycho-spiritual powers and holds their secret within, and according to the Veda, permeates everything in the Universe. Such names make it obvious that to the Vedic rishis, Agni is not an external fire but that of our innermost awareness and existence.

The transitions of Agni too are symbolic and yogic. As he grows in power, he becomes Mitra, the principle of love and harmony. As he grows wider, he becomes Varuna, the principle that permeates the whole Universe. And as Agni climbs higher, he grows into Indra, the luminous Mind above our usual station of though, and in its utmost ascent, unifies with *Savitra*, the Sun, the source and creator of the Universe. This may perhaps be considered as an earlier version or depiction of Kundalini Yoga in brief. To anyone with the slightest sense of the hidden movements of psychology, Agni then becomes a spiritual symbol that is not just poetry. He is a reality, an experience that grows in intensity as one grows inwardly, creating heat that is eventually felt physically, the *tapas* that is the energy of one's *Adhyatma*. Eventually, it is the *tejas* that is the immense power that the rishis invoked from the Sun, their own highest consciousness, possible to them with a revolutionary psychological transformation and rise.

In *Indian Philosophy: A Critical Survey*, Chandradhar Sharma notes that "the Vedic sages were greatly intellectual and intensely spiritual personages who in their mystic moments came face to face with Reality and this mystic experience, this direct intuitive spiritual insight overflowed in literature as the Vedic hymns." This is the right understanding of Agni and its direct perception in our consciousness.

Sri Aurobindo on Agni

Sri Aurobindo, in *The Secret of the Veda*, gives us a beautiful rendition of Agni,

> Agni in the Veda is always presented in the double aspect of force and light. He is the divine power that builds up the worlds, a power which acts always with a perfect knowledge, for it is jātavedas, knower of all births, viśvāni vayunāni vidvān—it knows all manifestations or phenomena, or it possesses all forms and activities of the divine wisdom. Moreover, it is repeatedly said that the gods have established Agni as the immortal in mortals, the divine power in man, the energy of fulfilment through which they do their work in him. It is this work which is symbolized by the sacrifice.

Agni is characterized by three main functions according to Sri Aurobindo. He is the *Purohita*, the officiant, and the face of Truth and *yajna*; the *Ritvik*, one who loves the bliss of Truth; and the *Hotar*, the one who invokes the Truth to establish itself in our lives.

Sri Aurobindo adds,

Psychologically, then, we may take Agni to be the divine will perfectly inspired by divine Wisdom, and indeed one with it, which is the active or effective power of the Truth-consciousness. This is the obvious sense of the word kavikratuḥ, he whose active will or power of effectivity is that of the seer—works, that is to say, with the knowledge which comes by the truth-consciousness and in which there is no misapplication or error. The epithets that follow confirm this interpretation. Agni is satya, true in his being; perfect possession of his own truth and the essential truth of things gives him the power to apply it perfectly in all act and movement of force. He has both the satyam and the ṛtam.

Moreover, he is *citraśravastamaḥ*; from the *Ritam* there proceeds a fullness of richly luminous and varied inspirations which give the capacity for doing the perfect work. For all these are epithets of Agni as the *hotṛ*, the priest of the sacrifice, he who performs the offering. Therefore, it is the power of Agni to apply the Truth in the work (karma or *apas*) symbolised by the sacrifice, that makes him the object of human invocation. The importance of the sacrificial fire in the outward ritual corresponds to the importance of this inward force of unified Light and Power in the inward rite by which there is communication and interchange between the mortal and the Immortal. Agni is elsewhere frequently described as the envoy, *dūta*, the medium of that communication and interchange.

The Imagism of Agni

The image of Fire is a poet's delight. It is a cornucopia of images, metaphors, and allusions, or as Ezra Pound might have said, a 'vortex.' Or as Stéphane Mallarmé waxed eloquently about the symbol, that it is not an abstract but a reality, beyond our subjective or objective differentiations.

To the Vedic seers then, Agni was not a dry image, but something alive, mysterious, luminous, with colors and emanations, forms and visions, tongues, and voices, leaping out to their pristine psychology, as to a child everything appears new, fresh, magical. It is not a world-weary philosopher looking at what he has already thought about and exhausted in his mind, but a wondrous, lively, passionate, and dynamic dazzle of things to a mind that is innocent and open. Agni to the rishis was an intense and obvious Reality, full of ardor and life. And that is who they were, the singers of this Agni.

Why is Agni such a perfect symbol for *Atman*? Because he is eternally pure. He is everywhere in various forms. He is mysterious, resplendent; without fixity, in shape or nature. Agni is not matter, nor abstract. He is within and without, connecting us with the Cosmos. He is also a primordial archetype with intricate psychological and emotional significance. Agni is the revelation that is constantly with us and is us, without a second. In our conception, the Divine is eternally pure. Thus, no matter what we throw in Agni it remains unsullied and purifies all that is offered or thrown in. That is why there is no duality in his being. Other *panthas* may need to contort themselves to protect or separate God from evil and keep the two apart. The true Divine contains all and has no need for duality of thought. And Agni is not just a symbol, he is a Deva, a force and power, an emanation and manifestation of the *Paramatman*. He responds to our *yajna* as a Divine Person. For *Paramatman* is not just impersonal but intimately personal. This insight is what makes its symbolism unique.

For this, Agni can be ecstasy, or longing, desire or passion, touch or burning, fever or transformation, lightning, or the Sun's flare. As a single flame, it is an eye. As multiple flames, it is innumerable tongues. It is the Unifier, the protector, the Invoker, the Leader, the Organizer, the Secret, the *Tapasvi*, the Poet, the Devourer, and the Guardian, the Messenger, the hidden Heart, the Offering, the Sacrifice, the Gift, or one's own Self. It can be divine and human, pure and beneficent, inspiration, and a kindling. It is presence, the center, the hidden spark of the eye or soul, the light in things, the history of man still alive in us, the psychic, the conscious, and so many more impressions to a rapt attention.

Thus, the sacrifice to Agni is not just external but an inner offering and oblation to the Divine within, and not just of external objects and delicacies but of all one's actions, movements, thoughts, feelings, etc. It has innumerable interpretations and none of them are wrong. He is the first Deva and key to the Veda.

Ghrtam or the Offering to Agni

Ghrta is usually taken as ghee, the purified butter, that was a special invention of the Indian civilization. Historians think this was done because of the hot weather of the subcontinent, and purifying the butter helped preserve it longer. It is also called Liquid Gold for its properties of clarity, color, taste, and fragrance, its great value in Ayurvedic concoctions and multiple health benefits. It is one of the five healthiest, balanced *satvik* or harmonious foods in Ayurveda.

I believe that these properties and the fact that ghee was an inalienable part of the Indian culture, its applications such as in eye drops, massage treatments, culinary arts and medicinal formulations, and its quality to break down only at a very high temperature, made it a special ingredient as part of the *samagri* of the yajnas (*samagri* means collection of materials or totality, completeness in Sanskrit).

But at another level, *ghra* means sprinkling. Sayana, the ancient Sanskrit scholar, also describes it as light. Yaska also considered it to mean fertilizing rain. But *ghra* also means to shine according to *The Practical Sanskrit-English Dictionary* by Vaman Shivram Apte. According to the *Cologne Digital Sanskrit Dictionary* and *Yates Sanskrit-English Dictionary*, it also means illumined. It can also mean spirit, energy (*tejas*). In Kannada, it means ardent devotion or enthusiasm.

In his *Notes on Root-Sounds*, Sri Aurobindo described the psychological significance of alphabets or *aksharas*: *Gha* implies a strong motion, *ri* signifies vibration and play and *ta* is touch or impact (that is light). The word *ghrta* gives a sense of a dense clarity and lucid play of light that touches one gently but impactfully.

The Fire that burns without smoke, Agni, is fed by the clarity, light, illumination, and energy of *ghrta*. If we accept the sense of Agni as the Divine presence within and the quiet flame within the heart, that is limpid and pure, offering *ghrtam* to it, which is one's own luminous and crystalline lucidity, to help it grow makes poetic and psychologic sense. Thus, the hidden meaning of pouring *ghrtam* in Agni is growing, strengthening, sustaining, and spreading one's consciousness wide in Yoga.

In fact, an inner silence, dense and transparent, full of devotion and as an offering to the sacred heart within, is one of the best ways to grow spiritually. *Ghrtam* thus becomes more than ladles of butter poured in a sacrificial rite. It is a profound depiction of what transpires within when the seeker becomes dense with clarity.

And it is fitting that *Ghrtam* relates to *Gau* subliminally in the human mind, the word *Gau* meaning both a cow and a ray of light, among other things. Or to put it in another way, when clarity of thought meets the intense revelation of Agni, one can experience new levels of consciousness and inspiration. Anyone who has the slightest experience of the art of meditation, prayer, dhyana, or yoga, would be able to relate to this insight.

In *Hymns to the Mystic Fire*, Sri Aurobindo luminously describes the same with far greater detail, definition, and radiance:

> The word ghṛta means ghee or clarified butter and this was one of the chief elements of the sacrificial rite; but ghṛta could also mean light, from the root ghṛ to shine, and it is used in this sense in many passages. Thus the horses of Indra, the Lord of Heaven, are described as dripping with light, ghṛta-snu—it certainly does not mean that ghee dripped from them as they ran... Evidently this sense of light doubles with that of clarified butter in the symbolism of the sacrifice. The thought or the word expressing the thought is compared to pure clarified butter, expressions like dhiyaṁ ghṛtācīm, the luminous thought or understanding occur.

If we take Agni as the Seer-Will, *kavikratuh*, then a crystal-clear state of consciousness needs to be poured constantly into its flame, to remove any turbidity or obstruction of gaze. Then suddenly, the meaning of the seventh verse of Mandala 1, Sukta 1 of the *Rig Veda* begins to make sense:

उप त्वाग्ने दिवेदिवे दोषावस्तर्धिया वयम् ।
नमो भरन्त एमसि ॥७॥

> To thee, O Fire, day by day, in the dawn and in the dusk, we come bringing to thee by the thought our obeisance (Translated by Sri Aurobindo)

Dr Tulsi Ram translates it thus, "Agni, lord omniscient, day by day, night and day, with all our heart and soul we come to you bearing gifts of homage in faith and humility." But the inner sense in his translation grows hazy for *dhi* (as in *Buddhi* and *samadhi*) is not heart and soul but a holding in mind and thought, a *dharana*, a focus of awareness that is steady and centered. The poet here is describing how he is meditating on the inner fire, his own divinity in the dedication of all his thought.

Mata Savita Joshi translates it into Marathi which translated tentatively into English, would mean, "O all-seeing and omnipresent, Divine, who should be worshipped. While doing everything, even one moment do I not forget you... With a firm and steady will I desire only the witness of all, who is everywhere, the Supreme Divine." In her simple manner she has described the content of the shloka.

The Agni Suktam: A Translation by Sri Aurobindo

This is the first hymn of the Veda and is an apt introduction to the sacred canon. A hymn of praise, welcome, and prayer to Agni, Lord of *Tejas*, composed when the mind of the Yogin Madhuchchhanda was full of *sattwic* energy and illumination, according to Sri Aurobindo:

1. Agni the brilliant I adore who standeth before the Lord, the god that has the ecstasy of the truth, the fighter that fulfilleth utter bliss.
2. Agni adorable to the sages of old, adorable to the new, holds up the gods with force and might.
3. By Agni one enjoyeth strength, one enjoyeth increase day by day and a mastery full of force.
4. O Agni, the Lord below about whom thou art on every side a flame encompassing, came by the gods into this world.
5. Agni the fighter, the strong in wisdom, the true, the manifold, the high of fame, has come to us, a god meeting with gods.

6. O beloved, that to the foe who would destroy thee thou,
O Agni, doest good, this is the Truth of thee, O Lord of
Love.

7. O Agni, to thee yearning if day by day we embrace
thee with our mind and bear the law, then thou
growest in mastery and might.

8. To thee the shining one of the gods below who
guardest the energy of the nectar and increasest in
thy home.

9. Do thou therefore, O Agni, become lavish of thy
approach to us as a father to his child; cleave to us for
our heavenly bliss.

Now that one has the key to the meaning and symbolism of
Agni, this *suktam* above might make coherent sense. Nalini
Kanta Gupta in his essay "A Commentary on the First Six Suktas
of Rig Veda" points out that

> [T]he first three *riks* (of this *Sukta*) deal with the theme:
> Who is Fire, what are his particulars, name and form?
> The second three deal with the subject: What is Fire, what
> his virtue, nature and innate tendencies? The third group
> describes the relationship between Fire and the aspirant
> in the manner of spiritual practice, the holy sacrifice.

One may also note here that the translation by Sri Aurobindo
attempts to capture the vibrations of the original in an utterly
alien language. It is extremely difficult to be sensitive to the
nuances and subtle echoes of Sanskrit and yet bring out all the
multiple meanings that the original hints at. Essentially, it is
a yogic rendering of the symbols of ancient hymn where the
spiritual sense is completely retained, for one who has the eye
for its subtle and cryptic layers. It is one of the most satisfying
translations of the *Agni Suktam*.

13

Indra: The Luminous Mind

Indra is seen as a god equal to Zeus or Thor. Wielding the thunderbolt, king of the gods, used to inconstancy and amorous relationships, while battling his enemies, the Titans, he seems like the other great gods of Greek or Roman pantheon in the *Puranas*. However, Vedic psychology is different.

To the Vedic seer, there is the world within, with its own earth and skies, its oceans and heavens, and wind and Sun. But these are not just mirror images of the external world. The inner world was more real to the rishis, while the outer and physical only an aspect or reflection of the internal. Thus, the inner space was *antariksha*, literally the inner eye, the space within. And the individual could ascend the planes of consciousness and the worlds within, which had their own science and order. It is this inner world they studied deeply and mastered and shared with us. While they did not disparage the outer, and the outer being was only a manifestation of the inner, mastery of the inner was a prerequisite to commanding the outer.

Thus, in the higher skies of the mind, as one ascends, one feels one's consciousness grow wider, more luminous, and clearer. There are various gradations to the hierarchy of the mental planes as one rises above. And Indra is the higher and luminous mind, without whom no spiritual transformation is possible. Or to put it in another way, man being a mental creature must use the help of his higher mind to begin the process of metamorphosis of his lower members.

Indra is not a concept but an actual principle and reality. His *vajra*, literally diamond, is the illumination from above that our mind receives as it comes in contact with Indra. He brings the higher consciousness to the vitality of the human, and without him, no spirituality is possible. Indra is endowed with *Vidyut Agni*, the Lightning Fire. And as Agni ascends the planes of consciousness, his fire is converted into an electric energy that empowers the universe and pervades the whole being.

In a ritualistic sense, Indra is the Lord of rain and lightning. In an inner spiritual sense, he is our own higher reality that unveils itself as we drop our identification with the lower energies. It is a symbolic revelation to realize that Agni is secretly the same essence as Indra.

Indra is widely described in the *Rig Veda* as one of the most important powers and devas. It is his lightning illuminations that remove the darkness that blocks our growth, the monster called *Vritra* who obscures our clarity by his oppressive stranglehold on our development. This too makes sense in the psychological interpretation since the higher mind is needed to remove any obfuscations and obstructions in our psychology. These dark blockages are a fact of spiritual journeys, and *Vritra* the concealer is the enemy that is vanquished by Indra to help us in our journey and ascent.

Indra in *Nirukta*

The linguistic roots of Indra are various and there is no clear consensus. It may be derived from *ind + u*, which means raindrop. Or the word *Ind*, which means equipped with great power. Or *idh*, which means to kindle. Or the root *Indha*, which means igniter, implying the light and power igniting *prana*, as in the Sanskrit word *Indhan*, meaning fuel. It could also have come from *idam* and *dra*, which would mean 'seeing this.' This much is clear, however, that the word *indri* means senses even now in Sanskrit and Hindi, not just our gross senses but also our subtle senses, for *dri-* means to see. It seems reasonable to see Indra as the Lord of the *indriyan*, or the sense-mind, with the senses being physical or non-physical, gross, or subtle.

Indra to me is also closely related to *antara*, which means the internal. Indra being the Lord of the internal world would then make sense. From *antara* comes the word *antariksha*, the inner space, literally the internal eye, as noted earlier, which is commanded by Indra, the higher mental consciousness. The trinity of Agni, Indra, and Surya is highly esteemed in the Veda, what in our psychological reading would mean to us as the inner being, the higher luminous mind and, finally, the superconscious, respectively.

Indra is not absolute existence as he is the Lord of *bhuvah*, the intermediate world between the earth and the *svara* or Sun-world. He is friendly to the seeker and not antagonistic or hard like the God of certain monotheistic religions using fear and punishment to affect behavior. He is effective and impactful, and his actions produce results. There is also a playful and vibratory quality about him. Perhaps these root sounds of its *Nirukta* may be used in further research to understand more and more the word-meanings and sense of related Sanskrit words.

The three worlds described in the Veda are *bhu*, *bhuvah*, and *svara*, i.e., the earth, the sky or atmosphere, and the realm of the superconscious. Indra is the awareness we meet as our own in *bhuvah*, the intermediate region, as we ascend from the earthly planes to the rarer, thinner atmosphere of the higher mind.

Indra is also described as *Vrishabha* in the Rig Veda. Literally, *Vrishabha* means the bull. To me, this means the immense power of the higher mind to effect change in us and to remove all obstructions in our growth and understanding. But *Vrishabha* is meant here also as a metaphor, just as *gau* (cow) and *ashva* (horse) in these hymns and would imply the powerful and vigorous male principle. It is interesting that *varsha* (the rain) comes from the same root as *vrsan*. And *Vritra*, the concealer and antagonist of Indra, too shares the same root as *Vrishabha*. According to Sri Aurobindo, the bull might be the earliest reference to the *purusha*, the pure consciousness of Sankhya that is untouched, unblemished, eternally free, and aware (as noted in chapter 5).

The Colloquy of Indra and Agastya (*Rig Veda* I.170)

This hymn illustrates beautifully the relationship between our aspiration towards rapid enlightenment and the need for the fullest development of the being prior to such an ascent:

Indra

1. It is not now, nor is It tomorrow; who knoweth that which is Supreme and Wonderful? It has motion and action in the consciousness of another, but when It is approached by the thought, It vanishes.

Agastya

2. Why dost thou seek to smite us, O Indra? The Maruts are thy brothers. By them accomplish perfection; slay us not in our struggle.

Indra

3. Why, O my brother Agastya, art thou my friend, yet settest thy thought beyond me? For well do I know how to us thou willest not to give thy mind.

4. Let them make ready the altar, let them set Agni in blaze in front. It is there, the awakening of the consciousness to Immortality. Let us two extend for thee thy effective sacrifice.

Agastya

5. O Lord of substance over all substances of being, thou art the master in force! O Lord of Love over the powers

of love, thou art the strongest to hold in status! Do thou,
O Indra, agree with the Maruts, then enjoy the offerings
in the ordered method of the Truth.

Indra is invoked by Sage Agastya in this extremely significant
shloka to assist in his journey towards immortality. This
invocation of the higher and luminous mind then would make
sense considering our paradigm and symbolism of Veda. Indra
insists that Agastya may not bypass him in his ascent and
agrees to provide help to the sage in his quest for a higher life.
This too is completely appropriate and would make sense to
anyone who understands human psychology and spirituality.
A poetic translation by Sri Aurobindo of their dialog captures
this dynamic between the human aspiration and the *daivik*
correspondence and both are critical for any spiritual endeavor.
Indra is not separate from us even though he appears far above
in the higher mind. He is only our higher self, manifesting at
another level of being.

Sri Aurobindo explains this remarkable hymn,

The governing idea of the hymn belongs to a stage of
spiritual progress when the human soul wishes by the
sheer force of Thought to hasten forward beyond in order
to reach prematurely the source of all things without full
development of the being in all its progressive stages of
conscious activity. The effort is opposed by the Gods who
preside over the universe of man and of the world and a
violent struggle takes place in the human consciousness
between the individual soul in its egoistic eagerness
and the universal Powers which seek to fulfil the divine
purpose of the Cosmos.

Finally, Agastya realizes his error and agrees to the partnership of
Indra to fulfill his *yajna*. This is the negotiated and incremental

spiritual progress, in harmony and cooperation and not in disunity or segregation with its divided energies. The human and the divine collaborate rather than compete or engage in conflict. This approach is unlike that of Greek mythology where the gods conflict with humans, as in the example of Prometheus mentioned in chapter 12. Here, there is no fire to steal; it is already within you and is you.

This is the importance of Indra. Not a transcendent God who threatens us with punishment if we do not obey, who is a 'schoolmaster of souls,' as Blake said, who treats us from his far heights as subjects. He is a collaborator and close partner in the human-divine endeavor to attain truth and immortality. And this is the next great insight from the Veda. God is not someone transcendent and far from us, an outsider who created this world by fiat and decree, whose orders must be obeyed in order to win a reward in some 'postmortem salvation,' but rather an integral part of us, our highest Truth and reality and our aspiration and goal, not just transcendent but also immanent, cosmic, and individual.

Indra and Sarasvati

With this insight, the assistance to Indra provided by Sarasvati makes sense. Sarasvati, as the name implies, is the one who is overflowing. The term was also used for an ancient river, it seems, in Indic history. But, as with all of Veda, each word has a mystical as well as a psychological basis and significance. Thus, Sarasvati is the divine inspiration that appears as the mind discovers its purity, elevates its movements to a higher platform, concentrates its energies into the luminous Agni, and prepares itself for the descent of the higher mental consciousness of Indra.

Literally, *rasa* is the joy that comes when the higher consciousness comes in touch with physical or sensual objects. Sarasvati is the ruler of all contact with the world, the bliss of experience, the *ananda* of touch.

According to Sri Aurobindo, Saraswati means

> She of the stream, the flowing movement, and is therefore a natural name both for a river and for the goddess of inspiration.... She is the current which comes from the Truth-principle, from the Ritam or Mahas, and we actually find this principle spoken of in the Veda—in the closing passage of our third hymn for instance.... We see in the third hymn (of the first Mandala) the close connection between Saraswati and this great water.... Saraswati is the Word, the inspiration, as I suggest, that comes from the Ritam, the Truth-consciousness.

Since Sarasvati is the inspiration from the highest consciousness of Truth, she is able to give Indra the strength to remove all obstructions of mind in the myth of Vritra.

Indra and the *Dasyus*

Similarly, one may understand the *Dasyus* too in this light given by Sri Aurobindo. *Dasyus* or the ancient devils are the negative formations that block the growth of an individual, the obstructions, *vighnas*, or blocks that the modern world of Jungian psychology would perhaps relate to, the dark side that Jung named as our Shadow. The forces of obscurantism, darkness, and deviance are well known to adepts of all spiritual and theological paths, and are variously called the devil, satan, *shaitan*, *ahiraman*, etc.

These are not Dravidians and the mention of the *Dasyus* does not in any way prove the fanciful Aryan Invasion Theory. This mis-identification of the *Dasyus* with the Dravidians is erroneous and based on poor scholarship with no evidential bearing or significance.

The various terms used for the *Dasysus* are *Vrikas* (the tearers), *Panis*, *Namuchi*, *Dasas*, *Danavas*, etc. Indra with his thunderbolt removes the obstacles they create, recovers the light they have hidden, and opens up the path of the truth that the rishis attempted to discover and travel on. And left as their trail.

14

Surya: The Truth, Existence, and Bliss

Surya is the symbol of the highest reality in Vedic psychology. It is not just the physical Sun, as we have noted with the Vedic devas, but the highest consciousness possible to man. Surya is the symbol of *sat-chit-ananda*, truth-consciousness-bliss.

According to Joseph Campbell in *Oriental Mythology: The Masks of God*, the word Surya is derived from Sanskrit *Su*, which means strength and power. But Surya means much more than that. He is the Lord of the *Svara loka*, the region above the sky in our inner space. The word *Svara* comes from *Sva*, which means the Self. And the word Surya may be derived from *Svara* or *Sura* in its *Nirukta*. The base *Sur* is cognate with Ancient Greek *helios*, Latin *sol*, Persian *khur*, and *Sur* from Proto-Indo-Iranian, which may come from Proto-Indo-European *soh₂wl*.

Surya is not just the source of energy to the material universe. He is seen as the creator, and as *Rohit*, the one who rises at dawn, red with his first rays. As *Pushan*, it is he who nourishes. As *Bhaskar*, the one who creates or gives light. As *Savitar*, he who impels. He is Mitra-Varuna, the friend and wideness of being. He is *Ushas*, or dawn. And he is Agni in all its forms. But he is also our highest possibility, the Source of the Universe. And the Vedic seers explored the various levels of consciousness within and found that the Sun is the external symbol for that *loka* or region where Truth is not separate from Existence in a perfect unity of being. Where the bliss of existence is innate to the being.

Surya is the symbol and deva of the complete unity of the cosmos, from where the rays spread to create the universe and get diffracted as in a prism into the various colors of the spectrum. Just as the various wavelengths of its light get broken into the various components, Consciousness too from its original oneness gets diffracted into the manifestations at different layers in Vedic hierarchy, until it becomes the complete and dense inconscient beneath us where no awareness is noticeable.

This truth of the Sun was called *sat* by the rishis, that which is eternally and universally unchanged and existent. It is this *sat* that manifests in the world and gives us the key to what is right, *ritam*, in thought, speech, and action. Surya thus, is a principle of what Sri Aurobindo calls the Supramental Consciousness, that which is full of harmony and a sense of integrality, where there is no contradiction, and the will is not separate from a global awareness and knowledge.

The Sun as the highest principle of existence is also seen in the times of Akhenaten, the Egyptian pharaoh who reigned from 1351–1334 BCE according to *Ancient Egypt*, edited by Mar Valls and Alberto Hernandez. He is depicted in relief as seated with his wife Nefertiti with the Solar Disc above him from which rays spread out. It is not known though whether his religious policy was absolutely non-dual or even monotheistic or not.

If we understand the Vedic mythology that reflects its psychology, then it makes sense that Agni is in essence the same as Surya and Indra, as discussed earlier in chapter 12. The *Jada Agni* is the same as *Saurya* or Solar Agni and also the same as *Vaidyut* or Lightning Agni of Indra. Thus, Surya is an experience and a realization to the Vedic seers, and they attempted to bring its light and consciousness not only down to the mind but also the vital and the body. This is their unique contribution to human spirituality, the key to which was lost for the last few millennia with *Kali Yuga* or the Iron Age.

The Sun in his chariot is driven by *asvas*, which are not physical horses but the energy of *Tapasya* or askesis. Its rays are described as *gau*, which may mean cows or rays of light. And with the arising of the Sun in the consciousness comes *Usha*, the dawn, in an eternal cycle of awakenings that have been celebrated in the Rig Veda.

As noted earlier, *Gau* in the Veda is not a cow, although one of the meanings of the Sanskrit term may mean the bovine creature. But *gau* also means a ray of sunlight, as in *Gautama* or *Gavisthira*. The naturalist interpreters think that the Vedic rishis are seeking a bounty of cows through their sacrifice. Yet, if we take this meaning of the word, then most of the Veda makes no sense, e.g., in hymns of the *Angirasa* tradition where the rishi attempts to discover the *gau* buried under the rock or where the Sun is radiating *gau* or where the *gau* is leading the *ashva* or the energy of askesis or *tapasya*.

Gautama is not a black cow if we take *gau-* as a cow and *tama-* as darkness, but it is one who is filled with light (*gah* + *tama* here imply the utmost light). Similarly, *Gavishthira* means someone who is established in the light (*gavah* + *sthira*). The words *gopuram*, *gochara*, Gauri, *goshti*, gaurav, *Gomati*, *Gayatri*, etc., imply the same significance of the word *gau* and are still used in Sanskrit and Prakrit languages. *Gau* thus, is an important symbol to understand the workings of Surya in our inner lives, and on a universal scale.

Joel P. Brereton and Stephanie W. Jamison in *The Rigveda: A Guide*, emphasize the significance of 'Dawn's ruddy cows as rays of light.' And Tatyana Elizarenkova in *Language and Style of the Vedic Rsis* complements this understanding by demonstrating that 'the cow symbolizes Sacred Speech.'

Similarly, *Usha*, the dawn, the first devi of the Veda, is not just a natural phenomenon. *Usha* is the dawn of human consciousness, the awakening of sensual and vital and mental man to something above, something radiant that brings to him newer horizons and vistas of beauty, light, revelation, awareness, and enlightenment. She is not just a physical dawn, but the opening of the individual and the global consciousness, a cyclic recurrence in the play of day and night. She brings with her Surya, the Solar rising, and is the propitious time when the invocation of Agni is performed.

Surya as Symbol of *Tad Ekam*

The famous shloka of the *Rig Veda* V.62.1 describes the experience of the kavi where he sees the Sun *as Tad Ekam*, That One, where all the rays are unyoked, and the majesty and might of the Divine is seen in its fullest plenitude. It is this same experience that is articulated in a similar manner in the *Isha Upanishad*, *shloka*s 15-16.

Similarly, the Gayatri mantra celebrates the grandeur of the Sun and has been chanted for time immemorial by spiritual seekers as the most important mantra of their *sadhana*. That Sun whom we adore and worship, the One of Divine effulgence and Truth on whom we meditate, is invoked to impel, and impregnate our minds. It is essentially an invocation to the Divine Truth-Consciousness to descend and assume and be the activator and energizer of our mental movements.

ॐ भूर्भुव॒ स्सुव॑ः
तत्स॑ वि॒तुर्व॑रेण्यं॒
भर्गो॑ दे॒वस्य॑ धीमहि
धियो॒ यो न॑ः प्रचो॒दया॒त् ॥ – Rigveda III.62.10

Here we give Sri Aurobindo's translation of the mantra, perhaps the best in English so far, "We choose the Supreme Light of the divine Sun; we aspire that it may impel our minds."

Sri Aurobindo explained: "The Sun is the symbol of divine Light that is coming down and Gayatri gives expression to the aspiration asking that divine Light to come down and give impulsion to all the activities of the mind."

Sri Aurobindo wrote his own Gayatri mantra in the tradition of a rishi passing on his own realization to humanity so that they may experience it too:

Om Tat Savitur Varam Rūpam Jyotih Parasya Dhīmahi Yannah Satyena Dīpayet

Let us meditate on the most auspicious form of Savitri, on the Light of the Supreme which shall illumine us with the Truth.

The Sun in Matter

One of the greatest achievements of the Vedic rishis was to realize that deep within the inconscient was hidden the same Sun in all its might and glory, self-hidden from itself, but arising from the depths of matter again in an upward ascent of spirit and consciousness. As Satprem describes in *Sri Aurobindo or the Adventure of Consciousness*, "[T]he Vedic Rishis, who were probably the first to discover what they called 'the great passage,' *mahas panthah* (*Rig Veda* II.24.6), the world of "the unbroken light," *Swar*, within the rock of the Inconscient.

"Our fathers by their words broke the strong and stubborn places, the *Angirasa* seers shattered the mountain rock with their cry; they made in us a path to the Great Heaven, they discovered the Day and the sun-world" (*Rig Veda* I.71.2). The Veda describes the discovery of the "Sun dwelling in the darkness" (*Rig Veda* III.39.5). And they sang in a strange modernistic symbol of "the treasure of heaven hidden in the secret cavern like the young of the Bird, within the infinite rock" (*Rig Veda* I.130.3).

The Veda described, "The contents of the pregnant hill (the material inconscient) came forth for the supreme birth... a god opened the human doors." (*Rig Veda* V.45). "Then, indeed, they awoke and saw all behind and wide around them, then indeed, they held the ecstasy that is enjoyed in heaven. In all gated houses (on all the planes of our being or in all the centers of consciousness) were all the gods" (*Rig Veda* IV.1.18). It is "the well of honey covered by the rock" (*Rig Veda*, II.24.4).

We have discussed this myth related in a modern direct language by Sri Aurobindo and the Mother, Pondicherry, when we studied their spiritual experiences.

Surya is not only the transcendent but also the immanent in Veda. There is no separation between God and man, *Nara* and *Narayana*, in essence. And the movement of spiritual growth is twofold: the ascent of Agni upwards, gathering with it all human energies, and movements in one concentrated rise, and the descent of the Sun and devas into the human being, facilitating there the alchemy and the transformation of the human *adhara*, or platform.

The famous *Agh Marshana sutra* (*Rig Veda* X.190.2-3) also describes clearly and precisely the creation of the Universe from the descent of the highest consciousness into the nescience and inconscient. The Surya then is the Supramental Consciousness descending into the night of the inconscient and involved in its dark. And as the Universe evolves through matter, life, mind, and then the higher levels, its rays or hidden *gau* re-emerge from the inconscient in a progressive unfolding as through the spectrum of the various *lokas*.

The Sun is the dispeller of the dark, which symbolizes ignorance. Indra, the higher Mind, uses the Sun's *ritam* and *tejas* to remove all obstructions of consciousness and destroy the dark force of *Vrika*. This in short is the essence of Surya, the highest potential that is still far above us and in the human condition almost as unthinkably and unimaginably distant as the mind is from matter. But who can yet be brought down to the human spheres as it was done by the Vedic seers in an individual capacity.

Sri Aurobindo translates *Rig Veda* I.50.10 thus, "Beholding the higher Light beyond the darkness we came to the divine Sun in the Godhead, to the highest Light of all."

He translates Yajurveda 17.67 thus, "I have risen from earth to the mid-world, I have risen from the mid-word to heaven, from the level of the firmament of heaven I have gone to the Sun, the Light."

Once one understands the hidden symbology, the linguistic systems, the literary device of *shlesha* and the ancient mindset, the mystery of Veda begins to unveil itself, in a consistent and comprehensive manner. As we descend deeper into the significance of the Surya, as not only Consciousness and its Force but also existence, we begin to understand the true relationship it has with Agni and the secret nature of Agni. For Agni as elaborated is not only a symbol but also a reality. It is our inner being, divested of all the impositions of our modern mind; it is our psychic, our sacred heart. It is our 'quiet still voice,' our *antahakarana*; it is the secret knower and the hearer of other dimensions.

If we realize that Consciousness and Energy, *Chitta* and *Shakti*, pervade everything, we have the secret formula of the Veda, the occult key to opening the great path again. And if we realize that consciousness is always a force, an action, a *Shakti*, then it is no longer seen as a passive quality, but a dynamic energizer and unifier of the whole cosmos. The Vedic Unity or Monism is not just a concept, created intellectually or in abstract, but a practical utility and a synoptic vision that combines all the diverse perspectives, like an ocean absorbing all the streams that flow into it.

15

Soma: The Concentration of Bliss

Soma is not an alcoholic drink or intoxicant, as some interpreters have assumed. Nor is it some special herb found in the Himalayas or some sort of mushroom or ephedra. It is the bliss of enlightenment, the delight of being that grows as Agni ascends upward and Indra becomes present to the normal awareness. It is the condensation of all the energies refined to their acme that appear with the revelations of the sunrays of knowledge and revelation. Soma is the *ananda* or bliss of *sat-chit-ananda* concentrating to a drop, *Indu*, and transforming the individual with a never-before tasted joy of life that makes everything else insignificant.

Soma also means the moon, and in the various disciplines to follow the Veda, such as Tantra and Yoga, it became a critical accomplishment once the seeker was prepared and made capable of holding the divine joy in his *dharana* or ability to sustain and focus consciousness. It is the elixir that drips as the highest distillate of purification and flows downward along the spine from the top of the vertex to fill the whole being—mind, vital, heart, and body—with *ananda*.

Soma is the extract of life. It is true that as the Yogi purifies himself with *tapasya* or Agni and askesis, the body's processes begin to transform and produce an innate joy of existing. Physiologically, this translates to an ecstasy without cause that exists organically, as a spontaneous by-product of a certain discipline in life.

The ninth mandala of the *Rig Veda* is dedicated entirely to Soma. And this is because of the central importance to this delight of being that Soma represents. Without this innate happiness, the vital energy or Vayu and the mind or Indra are not purified. Without their partaking of Soma, the rishi may not proceed with the *yajna*.

Agni as the *tapasya* is invoked in the first *sukta* of Mandala 1 of the *Rig Veda*. Its invocation and lighting up creates the Soma in the second *sukta* and Vayu and Indra are invited to drink and share in its ecstasy. Other devas such as Mitra and Varuna and the *Vishwadevas* (all-gods) are then invited to grow in the joy throughout the being and assist in the *yajna*. The symbolic nature of the entire exercise or ritual is clear and obvious.

David Frawley calls Soma the immortal nectar, the bliss of pure perception. In *Wisdom of the Ancient Seers,* he says, "Spiritual practice is maintaining and cultivating the Fire. The inner Fire is everything. It does not change anything but makes all things transparent, infuses all things with clarity, in which purity of perception Life reveals itself. The Flame of perception distils."

He adds perceptively, "The power of the transparent Flame of perception opens all things up and from that opening the essence comes forth, is extracted. Where there is direct observation, the essence effuses upwards from the heart that is everywhere. This essence is the Soma." Frawley has precisely described the yogic process by which Soma is generated in the body and spreads to the different parts and chakras in the various psycho-physical pathways that can be directly perceived.

The *Nirukta* of Soma

The origin of the word Soma is twofold. One is the Sanskrit *nirukta,* which consists of *su-* and *ma-*, the root sound *su-* implies good or beneficent or the Sun and *ma-* implies completion or fulfillment. Thus, Soma would mean a fulfillment that is healthy, wholesome, joyous, and full of light. It is also curious that in *Rig Veda,* IX.86.28-30, Soma is called the Sun itself and this seems etymologically appropriate. Soma also contains the sound Om, which to me is no mere coincidence as Om is the sacred word of the Vedic Universe of Sound. The other *nirukta* commonly offered is that Soma comes from the Sanskrit root *sav-su-*, which means to press. According to the *Monier-Williams Sanskrit-English Dictionary*, Soma means to "distill, draw extract or sprinkle." The cognate word in the *Avestan* is *haoma* but there it seems to have already taken a more physical significance.

Soma also means body in ancient Greek, which too is entirely apt since Soma is a physical physiological result of *kriyas* or processes in the body. Somatic is anything that relates to the body in modern English and biology.

Sri Aurobindo in *The Secret of the Veda* elaborates beautifully,

> Soma is the Lord of the wine of delight, the wine of immortality. Like Agni he is found in the plants, the growths of earth, and in the waters. The Soma-wine used in the external sacrifice is the symbol of this wine of delight. It is pressed out by the pressing-stone (*adri, graavan*) which has a close symbolic connection with the thunderbolt, the formed electric force of Indra also called *adri*. The Vedic hymns speak of the luminous thunders of this stone as they speak of the light and sound of Indra's weapon. Once pressed out as the delight of existence Soma has to be purified through a strainer (*pavitra*) and through the strainer he streams in his purity into the wine bowl (camū in which he is brought to the sacrifice, or he is kept in jars (*kalash*) for Indra's drinking.
>
> Or, sometimes, the symbol of the bowl or the jar is neglected and Soma is simply described as flowing in a river of delight to the seat of the Gods, to the home of Immortality. That these things are symbols is very clear.... Here, for instance, the physical system of the human being is imaged as the jar of the Soma-wine and

the strainer through which it is purified is said to be spread out in the seat of Heaven, divas pade.

Soma, Lord of Delight and Immortality (*Rig Veda* IX.83)

A hymn that symbolically describes the yogic process of Soma being prepared in the mind and body of the rishi:

1. Wide spread out for thee is the sieve of thy purifying, O Master of the soul; becoming in the creature thou pervadest his members all through. He tastes not that delight who is unripe and whose body has not suffered in the heat of the fire; they alone are able to bear that and enjoy it who have been prepared by the flame.

2. The strainer through which the heat of him is purified is spread out in the seat of Heaven; its threads shine out and stand extended. His swift ecstasies foster the soul that purifies him; he ascends to the high level of Heaven by the conscious heart.

3. This is the supreme dappled Bull that makes the Dawns to shine out, the Male that bears the worlds of the becoming and seeks the plenitude; the Fathers who had the forming knowledge made a form of him by that power of knowledge which is his; strong in vision they set him within as a child to be born.

4. As the Gandharva he guards his true seat; as the supreme and wonderful One he keeps the births of the gods; Lord of the inner setting, by the inner setting he seizes the enemy. Those who are utterly perfected in works taste the enjoyment of his honey-sweetness.

5. O Thou in whom is the food, thou art that divine food, thou art the vast, the divine home; wearing heaven as a robe thou encompassest the march of

the sacrifice. King with the sieve of thy purifying for thy chariot thou ascendest to the plenitude; with thy thousand burning brilliances thou conquerest the vast knowledge.

(Translated by Sri Aurobindo)

Once one gets the esoteric description, the entire verse is a beautiful description of the yogic process of experiencing the bliss of existence and the ecstasy of spiritual growth.

In *Rig Veda* VIII.48.3, the rishis make this powerful claim, "We have drunk the Soma, we have become the immortals: we have attained the Light, we have discovered the gods." This means either they had found a great principle or, as some Western interpreters think, were drunk. The only way to prove the former is to find the Soma within ourselves, imbibe the mysterious honey and wine of existence, and spread it around within and without.

16

Yajna: The Self-offering

Yajna is the central motif of the Vedic life. It is a profound understanding of the mysteries of existence and a poetic mythopoetic cosmogonic mystical journey to discover harmony, beneficence, joy, wellness, prosperity, and *amritam* or immortality in the world.

If we accept Agni as the symbol of the Divine Flame burning within, even intellectually, then the meaning of *yajna* becomes evident. *Yajna* is not a sacrifice in the sense that one is losing something precious. It is rather a gaining of something greater by purifying and cleansing something lower or less refined, as a transformation of one's composite parts; to propitiate and centralize and nourish the best within us. To choose a higher life of refinement and purity, self-culture, and elevation.

Traditionally, *yajna* has been called *karmakanda* (ritual works), but if we take our life in a deeper sense, all our works are an offering to the Divine and an action of the Divine, whether we realize it or not. Thus, the meaning of the term karma (works) may be apposite in describing the *yajna* as an offering of all our actions and activities to its holy resplendence.

The Meaning of Yajna

The word *yajna* (Sanskrit: यज्ञ, romanized: yajña) has its root in the Sanskrit *yaj* meaning 'to worship, adore, honour, revere' and appears in the early Vedic literature, composed in 2nd millennium BCE. (*Monier-Williams Sanskrit English Dictionary.*)

Sri Aurobindo explains the sense of the word in *Hymns to the Mystic Fire*,

> This word is of the utmost importance in the Veda. Its subsequent meaning of sacrifice has overclouded the sense of the Scriptures ever since the later half of the *Dwapara Yuga;* but originally and in the age of *Madhuchchhanda* it had no shade of this meaning. It is the root यज् with the suffix न adjectival.... यज् which had a sense of control, restraint, persistence, preservation... यज् means to regulate, rule, order, govern. यज is He who does these things, the Lord, Governor, Master, Provider, Giver, and in the Veda, it is applied to the Supreme Being, Parameshwara, who governs the universe as the Master of Nature, the Disposer of its Laws, the Almighty Providence, the Master of the Dharma.... यज: is formed by the addition of न, a nominal suffix which has the sense of action.
>
> यज्ञ therefore came to mean, he who rules, the governor or master; loving, adoring, also he who is loved; the means of mastery and so Yoga, in its processes, not in its realisations; the manner of mastery and so dharma, a rule of action or self-government; adoration or an act of worship.... In the ceremonial interpretation yajna is always understood as sacrifice and no other conception admitted. The Veda cannot be understood as the source of all Indian spirituality and divine knowledge, if this materialistic interpretation is accepted. In reality yajna is the name of the supreme Lord Vishnu himself; it also means dharma or yoga and by a later preference of meaning it came to signify sacrifice...

Kireet Joshi in *Glimpses of Vedic Literature* explains that the *Yajna* is "in its internal character, an act of self-offering so that the egoistic consciousness is abolished from all the psychological processes. The Vedic gods are... cosmic powers and beings representing different aspects of the one Ultimate Reality." It is *askesis, kenosis, catharsis,* and *ekstasis* all in one, the ascetic concentration, the purification, and the standing outside of oneself in the discovery of bliss.

Agni is the *ishta deva* of the heart center, according to ancient spiritual wisdom, where seated deep within it is an *ansha* or portion of the Cosmic and Transcendental Divine. It is the *jeevatman*, the self of the being that connects one to all the psychological principles and powers. The purpose then is to grow the fire that feeds on everything without discrimination or prejudice, and the *yajna* is this radical reversal of consciousness where one sees the Universe not with external eyes but from within.

This way of seeing the Divine within as the portion of the Divine in all is the seed of the Bhakti movement that followed the Vedic age in the legend of Radha and Sri Krishna and later the Bhakti tradition in medieval India, as noted earlier in chapter 5. But the *yajna* is not just the discovery of devotion and adoration but also the union of jnana, bhakti and karma, knowledge, worship, and works.

Read with this elemental key and the ones we have explored previously, the entire Veda will read in one flow, with consistency of symbolism, meaning, even rhythm and meter. To reiterate, it is a work of a highly civilized culture and community of seers who were also great poets, and we are only now beginning to acknowledge this radiant fact.

I believe it is open to anyone who is willing to study it even in translation. The time has perhaps arrived to open its occult secrets to anyone willing to look with intent and dedication.

We cannot go back to the Veda in its older version perhaps, as Swami Dayananda exhorted us. But we can certainly learn from it, immerse ourselves in its ancient psychology, linguistics, symbology, prosody, and explorations. Absorb it in our marrow. And perhaps adapt the lessons learnt to the modern life, collectively, for it belongs to all of us, just as the beautiful sermons of Christ, the luminous teachings of the Buddha, or the synthetic vision of Sri Krishna.

V

The Invocation

17

The Last Hymn of the Veda

Samvanana Angirasa Sukta X.191

1. O Fire, O strong one, as master thou unitest us with all things and art kindled high in the seat of revelation; do thou bring to us the Riches.
2. Join together, speak one word, let your minds arrive at one knowledge even as the ancient gods arriving at one knowledge partake each of his own portion.
3. Common Mantra have all these, a common gathering to union, one mind common to all, they are together in one knowledge; I pronounce for you a common Mantra, I do sacrifice for you with a common offering.
4. One and common be your aspiration, united your hearts, common to you be your mind—so that close companionship may be yours.

(Translated by Sri Aurobindo)

This is a very powerful message and advice for all of us: harmony, unity, shared purpose, comradeship, the aspiration for Truth, and experience of bliss. For the Veda was not just a superficial ritual to propitiate and please the gods to gain favors. It is our collective heritage and shared past. It belongs to all of us even as it took birth in the cradle of the Indic civilization. We all can learn from it, non-denominationally, as a single human family, which is how the ancient seers saw us—for it belongs to humanity and is universal.

But one needs to go beyond the present 'narratology' and open one's mind to alternative possibilities in our history. One must be able to question, and question profoundly, relentlessly, without bias or prejudices or agenda. For there is much in the Veda that is of value which we have forgotten, since we do not even realize what it said and was, and how, in many ways, we are still living the life and culture of the Veda.

The Veda is not just our past, but also our future. An awakening to its validity and relevance, that continues to this day in our lives, might be of crucial importance if we aspire to save our civilization and lead it to its future evolution. For it gave due emphasis to both—our hidden unity and our innumerable multiplicity—giving each its space and due place in the universal scheme of things, while bringing a synergy and harmony to both the poles of oneness and manifold variance. Its Unity is authentic to the extent it could allow each the utmost freedom and multiplicity of articulation and way of being. Because it allows the Divine *Paramatman* and each deva as a friend and partner in the journey of life, its monism is the true Monism—dynamic, alive, and eternal. Not the artifactually constructed and abstract concept of limited paradigms that allow no independence and are unable to embrace all in their partial sense of Oneness.

The Veda is a celebration and an affirmation of life and our divinity. It does not shirk from the world, as some later branches of Indian spirituality attempted to do with their emphasis on *Sannyasa* or renunciation of the world. It is an integral approach to every aspect of our condition and is a transformational alchemic mindset.

It is entirely possible that the Vedic cycle, that the rishis hinted at, has returned to raise humanity back to the eternal, universal, and infinite way of life, what the Indians call the Sanatana Dharma. If it has, then perhaps it is time once again to dust the palm leaves of our mind on which it lays inscribed but forgotten, and hear its ancient chant reverberate through our consciousness, in an eternally fresh resonance of our own highest and innermost truth.

Suggested Reading

A History of Sanskrit Literature by Arthur Anthony Macdonell

A New Approach to the Vedas by Ananda K. Coomaraswamy

A Theory of Semiotics by Umberto Eco

Elements of Semiology, Mythologies, S/Z, The Pleasure of the Text by Roland Barthes

From Veda to Kalki by Tommaso Iorco

Helgoland by Carlo Rovelli

Hymns to the Mystic Fire, The Secret of the Veda along with *The Complete Works of Sri Aurobindo*

Jung by Deirdre Bair

Language and Style of the Vedic Rsis by Tatyana Elizarenkova

Lights on the Veda and *Further Lights on the Veda* by T.V. Kapali Sastry

Morphology of the Folktale by Vladimir Propp

Rig Veda Bhasha Bhashya (in Hindi) by Swami Dayananda

Rig Veda Samhita by R.L. Kashyap

Selected Works of M.P. Pandit

The Complete Works of the Mother

The Idea of India Bharat as a Civilisation by Subhash Kak

The Obscure and the Mysterious: A Research in Mallarme's Symbolist Poetry by K.D. Sethna

The Rig Veda by Wendy Doniger

The Rigveda: A Guide by Joel P. Brereton and Stephanie W. Jamison

The Rigveda: The Earliest Religious Poetry of India by Stephanie W. Jamison and Joel P. Brereton

Wisdom of the Ancient Seers by David Frawley

Appendix I: Key Symbols of the Veda

These are the most significant symbols in the Veda to my mind, and in this section of appendices, we attempt to shed more light on them that may be of interest to students of semiotics. Understanding them gives one a deep insight into the vision of the rishis and makes the Veda simpler to understand, just like the twelve sutras discussed in chapter 4. We share an elucidation of these symbols to again allow the modern mind to scan through the vast ranges of Veda summarily and then return at leisure for a more elaborate learning.

Agni implies, as we have noted throughout the sections earlier, the Divine within, the psychic being that is the eternal and uninjurable (*anahata*) center of our life. Swami Dayanand called it the *Vachi* (speaker, representative, voice) of *Atman* and *Paramatman*, the Self and the Supreme Self. The Mother, Pondicherry, called it Divine Love. It is *tapas*, askesis, and the Divine Will within and without. Agni is the representative and the leader, who loves the Truth, the most prominent and eminent who connects us to all the other devas.

To reiterate, Agni is *agre netar*, the eminent one, the leader of our life who is ever in the forefront. He is *Jatavedas*, the knower of our births and lives, the indestructible (*a-gni*). Sri Aurobindo calls it the power of transformation. (The symbol of Agni has been discussed in detail in chapter 12 as part of the section "*Yajna* and the Fourfold Godhead of the Veda.")

To add to this symbolism, Agni has another meaning, according to Subhash Kak in *The Idea of India: Bharat as a Civilisation*. Agni is also *Vac* or speech. Kak explains,

Agni and Vac are two manifestations of the same deeper reality ... both reside in the waters and in trees. The waters of materiality hide the spark of Agni and the sounds of their waves; from trees comes fire as well as the wood for flutes and other musical instruments. There is a deeper connection between the elements of *tejas* (fire) and *vayu* (air)....Agni has two forms, the fierce Rudra and the auspicious Siva.

This is Kak's translation of the first *rik* of *Agni Suktam*: "I praise Agni, the priest (*purohita*) who is the light (*devam*) and the invoker (*rtvij*) of the sacrifice, whose chants (*hotr*) bestow treasure." Kak has taken the psycho-physical model used in Yoga and Tantra to explain the uniqueness of devas as they are represented, planted and established in the body with the invocations of mantra during *yajna*.

Gau is not cow, but the rays of sunlight or the knowledge that comes from the highest levels of consciousness or the Divine, as noted several times earlier as a point of emphasis throughout the book. Swami Dayanand took *gau* as the Sun itself in various mantras. According to David Frawley, the cow has multiple connotations including the mantra, the receptive mind, perception, knowledge, wisdom, the Earth, the sky, the dawn, a singer, a song, archetype, the mystery (*guh*), among others. Sayana too took *gau* as a sunbeam at times.

A.B. Purani in *Studies in Vedic Interpretation* says that it is incontrovertible that *gau* in the Veda means sunlight and higher knowledge. Words like *gopuram*, *goshti*, *gochara*, *gauri*, among others, used even today in Sanskrit and Hindi only confirm his statement. *M. Monier-Williams Sanskrit-to-English Dictionary* has multiple double-columned pages of meanings for the word *gau* or *go*, including 'herds in the sky' or 'stars.' (*Gau* has been discussed in detail in chapter 14 in the section "*Yajna* and the Fourfold Godhead of the Veda.")

Ashva is not a horse but vital energy or *prana* or chi. In the Veda the horses are led by the cow, which makes sense since the cow is the divine knowledge that is followed by pranic energy. *Ashva* is the energy that comes from *tapasya*, or askesis. It is the life force, the power generated by self-mastery and self-control; thus, the horses that pull the chariot of the Sun or the seeking of the *Ashva* by the Vedic rishis as they invoke Indra and make offerings to Agni.

Sampadanand Misra in *A Note on the Word Asva* has given us the etymology of the word *Ashva*:

> [The] root-sound *ash* which means to consume, to eat, to possess, to have, to obtain, to enjoy, etc. Because of this original sense, the word *ashva* derived from the root-sound *ash* also refers to the dynamic force of life, of vital and nervous energy. Originally, the word must have implied strength, speed, etc. The animal possessing much dynamic energy, swiftness was also referred to as *Ashva*. So, the meaning horse is secondary.... Here the word refers to the property or the quality of the object and not specific to a single object. Some other words derived from the same root are: *asman* (stone), *ashni* (thunderbolt), *ashri* (a sharp-edged weapon). All these words refer to strength, solidity, speed, sharpness, etc.

To this, we may add the word *anashana*, which is used even today in Sanskrit and Hindi, and means fasting or not eating.

Ghritam in Veda is not purified butter but clarity and brightness of mind that is essential for spiritual growth. Wendy Doniger in *The Rig Veda* feels that *ghritam* is a symbol of the original chaos of the Universe that is purified into creation, similar to how milk from the *gau* is churned and then purified into ghee. If so, she is pointing to the same clarity that *ghritam* comes to be in the Vedic verses. (The symbol *ghritam* has been discussed in detail in chapter 12 in the section "*Yajna* and the Fourfold Godhead of the Veda.")

Water or *apas* represents being or the movement of consciousness. For example, the ocean signifies the vastness of being. The Sarasvati river is inspiration from *Sacchidananda* who descends from the Sun. Crossing the ocean implies the spiritual journey.

Why is water an apt symbol for Being and Consciousness? Because it can take any form or state and yet remain unchanged. The vast ocean reminds us of infinity. The river of individual movement. Rain of divine blessing and knowledge. Water can be solid, liquid, or gas, but in all these phases it is still water. It can be in a cup, ponds or lakes, or other shapes, but it is still water. Such is the nature of *Chitta*. You may throw dirt in it, but its essence will always be pure. Water is a powerful Vedic symbol that survives with us even now.

The symbolism of water as existence or consciousness-energy recurs throughout the Veda and Upanishads and even today carries to us words such as *Bhavasagar*, the ocean of the Universe or Being, in Sanskrit and Hindi. (I have tried to bring out this symbol in the introduction to this book.)

Soma is not alcohol or an intoxicant, but the bliss that arises spontaneously through the process of Yoga, or through the intense purification wrought by Agni. This ecstasy of Soma is offered to the *prana* or Vayu, to the higher or luminous mind or Indra, and to all the devas. It purifies them and intensifies the Yoga taking away all distractions and dissipation. Soma is not just a symbol but also a Deva without whom yoga cannot proceed. Western researchers have written volumes of publications surmising that Soma is either an intoxicant, hallucinogen, entheogen, psychedelic, or stimulant. None of them appears to have the experiential understanding of Soma though. To see Soma as an external drug is a grave error of modern scholarship.

Subhash Kak in *The Idea of India: Bharat as a Civilisation* adduces,

> Soma represents the moon but also sometimes Visnu or even Siva (as Somanatha).... The pressing of the Soma is the purification of the mind, mirrored in the sacred theatre of the pressing of the herb that it makes possible to connect to the heart of one's being.

Soma is a very important touch point (literally) in the Veda and subsequent developments, such as Yoga, Tantra, Vaishnava Bhakti, and Indian mystical poetry. One of the earliest steps in the spiritual development of the seeker which gives them joy, health, rejuvenation, and the door to inner and higher worlds, it is also one of the most critical. (Soma has been discussed in detail in chapter 15 in the section "*Yajna* and the Fourfold Godhead of the Veda.")

Adri or hill or rock is the inconscient layer of our being and the Universe that still hides the highest consciousness within, for the Divine is everywhere. The myth of *Vala* is this recovery of Sun rays from the pit or *bila* of the rock, the dense darkness of Nescience.

Whenever *Adri* is mentioned in Veda as a hill to be climbed, it implies the spiritual journey upward, stage by stage, step by step.

Sky or *antariksha* is a symbol of the vital that has been discussed in the Vedic model of the Universe. Sky is also *Bhuvar*, and *Svar*, forming the trinity of *Bhu-Bhuvar-Svar* with earth, sky, and Sun-world. For the Universe reflects the microcosm of the individual. *Bhu* signifies the earth or physical consciousness.

There are many other skies in Veda as has been discussed in chapter 11. Besides *antariksha*, the word *dyau* too is used for the sky, but it is the higher sky of the mind, ruled by Indra or the devas. Above *dyau* comes the *Svar*, where the unity of the world begins to be seen and one approaches the lid or the door of the Sun, above which there are even higher worlds.

Then there is the *Parama Vyoma*, the Ultimate Space, where the mantra is born. This space is not physical but the consciousness of rishis where the mind ascends to the level of unity, bliss, and vastness that we conceive as the Divine.

Sun is a symbol of *sat-chit-anand*, our highest state of being and spiritual experience, the principle of unity and creation of the world. Sri Aurobindo took it to mean the Supramental principle which is Truth-Consciousness or *Rit-Chit* described in the Veda. But the Sun is not just a symbol. It is also a deva and an experience. Sun or Soorya is also *Savitar* and *Pushana*, who creates, energizes, and nourishes the Universe. He is the Godhead, *Ishvara*, the Divine Eye watching over the entire universe.

As the rishi ascends in awareness higher and higher, he directly apprehends the Sun or the Sun-consciousness and grows in the Light and Bliss of the Supermind. (Surya has been discussed in detail in chapter 14 in the section "*Yajna* and the Fourfold Godhead of the Veda.")

Ushas or Dawn is the symbol of spiritual awakening, individually and collectively, "the coming of the supramental Light...with its shining herds," as Sri Aurobindo explains in *The Doctrine of the Mystics*. That is why the rishi can make dawn happen by invocation and chanting of the mantra, which would not make sense if *Ushas* were only a physical phenomenon. *Ushas* is the first devi of the Veda. And it is interesting in the Veda how closely the Dawn is aligned with the Sun, both implying a similar symbology of light and awakening (the verb *vas-/us-* means to light up). The return of *Ushas* causes the birth of the Sun in the Veda. And the Sun chases *Ushas*, poetically and metaphorically as his beloved.

Kutsa Angirasa brings out the continuity and constant freshness of *Ushas* in this beautiful hymn,

She follows to the goal of those that are passing on beyond, she is the first in the eternal succession of the dawns that are coming, Usha widens bringing out that which lives, awakening someone who was dead.... What is her scope when she harmonises with the dawns that shone out before and those that now must shine? She desires the ancient mornings and fulfils their light; projecting forwards her illumination she enters into communion with the rest that are to come. (*Rig Veda* I.113.8,10, translated by Sri Aurobindo)

A deva can also be a symbol of a deep truth like Agni or Soma. But he is not just a concept or abstract. To the rishis the devas were real and alive, and the *yajna* was their invocation with specific concentrations and sound, manifesting the power of their names that made them appear, with the deep devotion and purity of Agni. According to Subhash Kak in *The Idea of India: Bharat as a Civilisation*, "*Devam*, (is) translated by Griffith as 'God' ...devas are the cognitive centres in the mind. The word 'God' is meaningless here excepting in its primary meaning of Light."

These symbols might appear gross to the superficial eye. But they are subtle and mysterious and to the rishis even thought was gross in appearance. An ancient mystery surrounds their invocation that takes our discursive modern mind away from the surface to a quiet invoked space resounding with hidden suggestions and echoes of the subliminal. It is refreshing to see how the Veda brings three aspects of language that are usually considered separate, semiotics, etymology and linguistics, together. For example, the root of the word Agni and its comparative linguistics imply the same eminence, force, and intensity that the visual image and poetic metaphor provide to our mind. Thus, sound, sense, and vision are unified into the subconscious; meter and prosody merge with the sign, and the ear and eye are not two separate senses. This can create a unique impact, unified and sacred, on the schizophrenic sensibility that modern linguistics offers us. (Umberto Eco called this the metaphor-pun in *A Theory of Semiotics*, but the Vedic symbol goes even further than his brilliant insight.)

Modern semiotics has not understood Vedic symbols. I believe that once that happens modern semiotics as well as linguistics will undergo a drastic and wholesome transformation. Roland Barthes famously showed the layers of meanings in the movie *Ivan the Terrible* by the means of signs, symbols, narrative, and subtler 'filmic' nuances that underlie the superficial textual and visual message in his essay "The Third Meaning." We will need a similar deep dive into the symbology of Veda going into how the symbol transforms our consciousness and penetrates to the core of our being if we learn to hold it in our awareness with stillness and openness.

Appendix II: Key Devis

Each devi, or the feminine aspect of the deva, is also a symbol, a metaphor, a yogic perception, and a spiritual experience, both intensely personal and impersonal, abstract as well as real. Here we discuss important devis with the same aspiration to present them before the modern mind in an elementary manner. This is to give an idea about the multiple significances of the symbols we take for granted in our lives. Hopefully, this will help turn them from surface images in our minds to multi-dimensional beings or realities. As Sri Aurobindo elaborates in *The Doctrine of the Mystics*, "...the Deva is both Male and Female and the gods also are either activising souls or passively executive and methodizing energies.... Each god, too, has his female energy."

1) Aditi is the Divine Infinite Mother, the undivided One, who created and is the Universe. The word Aditi is formed of two Sanskrit roots *adya-* or *adi-* and *ti-* which imply the First Light. Aditi is often misunderstood as only an abstract, as M.P. Pandit has pointed out in his essay "Vedic Deities". But Aditi is a living Reality to the Vedic sage, and it is thus that we should accept her.

2) Sarasvati, mentioned earlier in chapter 14 in the section "*Yajna* and the Fourfold Godhead of the Veda," is a devi but also a symbol of inspiration that descends from the highest states of the Sun-world. She brings down the light, knowledge, insights, wisdom that transforms our mind and assists Indra in opening the blockages in understanding. She is *Sruti*, the revelation of hearing, that overwhelms the mind with its puissance and brilliance. Sarasvati means 'she of divine *rasas* and essence of existence.' She is the great ocean of light above, *maho arnava,*

and not just a physical river. And she descends with seven rivers, each symbolizing the seven *lokas* of being.

3) Sarama or intuition leads Indra, or the luminous mind, to discover the hidden Sunrays or *Gau* that have been entrapped in *Adri* or the Rock of Nescience. She is one of the five powers of the Truth-Consciousness, higher devis that assist the mind in the *yajna*. The other four are Sarasvati, or the Divine Inspiration; Ila, or Divine Revelation; Mahi or Bharati; and Dakshina or Divine Discernment. These five devis are higher powers from ranges above the mind who bring down the truth to our mind and help us in our spiritual growth and journey. Sarama is not a 'bitch' as is popularly represented by Western commentators and analysts.

4) Gayatri is a devi, the most prominent and well-known meter in Veda, a *chhanda* and significant mantra that is recited even after thousands of years in the Indian peninsula by seekers. The word Gayatri means an instrument of going or reaching. The *chhanda* or metrical form consists of three padas or sections, each with eight syllables or *varnas*. The Gayatri Mantra composed by Sage Vishvamitra invokes the Unity of the Sun to impel and transform our minds (more detail on this in chapter 14 in the section "*Yajna* and the Fourfold Godhead of the Veda").

5) Ila is the devi of vision, "the strong primal word of the Truth," according to Sri Aurobindo. She, with Sarasvati, Dakshina, Mahi, and Sarama, are the five *shaktis* of divine inspiration and the descent of higher light on our minds. In the later developments of Purana, she is unified with Sarasvati and Sarama and is worshipped solely as Sarasvati. But in the Veda, she occupies a prominent place, the awakened power of sight, just as Sarasvati is the power of hearing.

6) *Ushas,* meaning Dawn or the awakening of consciousness, individual or collective. (Refer to Appendix I.)

7) *Vak* is the goddess of speech. Speech or the speech-act is of utmost significance in the Veda, for it signifies an awareness that is not separate from the will and is inspired and able to clearly articulate the greater vision. But *Vak* is also a Divine Force and Being who is worshipped and adored in the Veda, an expression of the One Reality that created the Universe from a primordial vibration, also called the *anahada nada*.

   Modern linguistics holds that the word and the thing it denotes are separate. That choosing the name for an object is wholly arbitrary. Vedic *bhasha gyana* holds that each root sound or *beeja dhvani* has its own *guna* or quality with its own psychological and metaphysical impact. And that this essential nature of sound connects the order of words and the order of things. Thus, inspired speech that is refined and arises out of a consciousness that beholds the truth is a great force and can effect a unique transformation in the individual and the listener. This is the secret of *Vak*, the devi of Veda who is also its inspiration and its manifestation. Her truth is that every utterance can be a "mantra" depending on the inspiration, intent, and power with which it is uttered.

8) Mahi is the devi of wideness, largeness of vision, and accomplishment, also known as Bharati. Bharati, as our previous discussion on Bharata in chapter 3 would suggest, bears the root of one who upholds the light of higher knowledge and wisdom. In the Puranic literature, Ila, Bharati, and Sarama are absorbed into Sarasvati, who becomes the devi of higher learning, wisdom, perfection in the crafts, and later, one of the four emanations of Maha Shakti.

9) Dakshina is the goddess of discernment, *viveka*. "Her function is to dispose the action and the offering and distribute in the sacrifice to each godhead its portion," as Sri Aurobindo has pointed out. The root word of Dakshina is *daksha-*, which implies right, balance, ability, and discernment.

Appendix III: Some Other Key Devas

1) Rudra is the fiery ascetic who brings in force to the Yoga and *yajna*. He appears fearsome and terrible but is benign and gentle. He is the Vedic progenitor of Shiva.

   Rudra is raw force and energy of *tapasya*, the one who is withdrawn from the evanescent attractions of the world. His purity, intensity, other-worldliness are yet essential to development in Yoga. In later Yogas, he becomes the inspiration for the mendicant, the *aghodis* and *kapalis*, and *nagas*, who detach from the world inwardly and outwardly, in a state of *sannyasa*. Shiva is the gentler, kinder, auspicious aspect of Rudra who is part of the trinity of Brahma-Vishnu-Shiva in the Puranas.

2) Vayu is the deva of vital energy. He is the key to sustaining all movement in Yoga, and without him there would be no creativity, impulse, passion, or force in the human life on earth plan.

   Once Vayu has tasted Soma he realizes the true bliss of life away from transient pleasures, is energized and purified and becomes an indispensable instrument in the spiritual journey of the *yajna*. This is brought out clearly in the second sukta of the first mandala and is a recurrent theme throughout the Veda.

3) Mitra is the deva of friendship, harmony, love, and goodwill. The term "mitra" in Sanskrit means friend. Without Mitra there is no maturity of the emotional mind and further growth in Yoga does not happen. Mitra, Varuna, Aryaman, and Bhaga are the four devas who are essential for the growth of our emotional mind, as Sri Aurobindo has pointed out in *The Secret of the Veda*.

4) Varuna is the deva who embraces and encompasses everything, the Lord of wideness, justice, and purity.

   Varuna is the one who embodies the Universe, pervades it all, and makes the emotional mind vast and capable of holding all opposites, contradictions, possibilities, and states. Without him there is no widening of the heart or its expansion to a wider base and foundation capable of holding the intensest bliss and knowledge.

5) Bhaga is the deva of enjoyment, the taste of *rasa*, or the essence of things. He is also the god of love. The word *bhaga* comes from roots *bha-* and *ga-*, which imply the impulsion of light. It also derives from the root *bhaj-*, which means to enjoy and share.

   The word *Bhagavan* means the Lord of Light and has the same roots as *Bhaga*.

6) Vishnu is the all-pervading Godhead. In the Puranas, he becomes the sustainer, and retains his eminence. Vishnu is the most important deva of the Veda and yet he is mentioned less frequently than Agni or Indra. For the seeker the most important devas in yoga are the latter two, since they are the ones that are of immediate help in our growth in daily endeavors. It is an error to think that just because less *riks* are dedicated to Vishnu he is less important than any other.

   It is only in the Puranas and latter-day Vaishnava Bhakti that Vishnu becomes the more prominent deva right from the beginning, and the stages of development from Agni to Indra and then to Vishnu are bypassed.

7) *Vishvadeva* means all-devas. The combined energy of all the manifestations of the One Reality, *Tad Ekam*. *Vishvadeva* is not a concept. It is a reality. For the unity of the devas is not an arbitrary compilation but is the key understanding in approaching the unity of the Universe.

   As we understand the concept and reality of *Vishvadeva*, we begin to come closer to the True Unity and Monism of the Veda. For the energies of the devas comes together into the one entity, which is invoked early in the first mandala. They are never antagonistic or disjointed. This essential unity recurs constantly throughout the Veda, depicted in *Tad Ekam* and in another symbol and experience through the invocation of *Vishvadeva*.

8) Ashwins are the devas of vital energy, who are healers, gods of youth and energy, and enable the body and mind to sustain the *yajna*. Ashwins are closely related to Vayu since both are associated with *prana* or vital energy. But Ashwins appear to work at a higher plane and Vayu on the plane of the mortals. Both are essential to impulsion in Yoga to newer stations and are transformed into *tapas* eventually.

9) *Martanda* is the Dark Sun. It literally means the 'dead egg.' Aditi, the mother of the devas, gave birth to eight Suns. The first seven were for the seven *lokas*. The eighth Sun was thrown in the dark inconscient and nescient. From there it awakens and rediscovers its hidden light and brings light into the darkness. According to R.L. Kashyap, *Martanda* is the Sun of the human world, where it sees life and death, and awakens humanity to its secret immortality.

10) *Brahmanaspati* or *Brihaspati* is the deva of the primal word that creates. He becomes Brahma in the later Puranas but retains his function as the creator. The word *Brahmana* originally meant the mantra, with its significance of generation and giving birth to spiritual forces or the devas.

11) Aryaman is the deva of right and intense work. Along with Bhaga, Mitra and Varuna, he helps the seeker grow in his emotional mind and become capable of yogic ascent in consciousness. "He is an immortal puissance of clear-discerning aspiration and endeavor," according to Sri Aurobindo.

Appendix IV: Some Key Concepts and Terms of the Veda

These key terms, often misunderstood, hold the secret to understanding the Veda along with the symbols, devas, and other sutras. These too have a profounder sense, more psychologically plastic and wide-ranging than modern commentators and interpreters have understood and presented. Words are not just random sounds with meanings in Veda. They are charged and inspired, each with deep feeling and meaning, and each of these words is not a concept but a lived experience and reality to the rishi.

Ritam is Truth in manifestation, one of the key terms in Veda. Tatyana Elizarenkova translates it as the Cosmic Law. She demonstrated how our understanding of the word has evolved over the last few decades. And how an understanding based on the translation of the word by Sayana has progressed from all kinds of confusing explanations to an appreciation closer to the original Indic thought. H. Grassman translated it as "divine order," "eternal truth," "justice," "right," "sanctity," "truth," "a pious deed," and "sacrifice." And he was closer to the mark than Sayana who translated it variously as "water," "sacrifice," "truth," "food," or "one who has gone," contorting the meaning of the verses to a ritualistic impression that transforms the Veda into a confused heterogeneous mass that has no consistency of meaning or sense.

Elizarenkova pointed out that "the dynamics of cosmology finds its reflection in the very etymology of the word *rta-*, a past passive participle of the verb *r-/ar-*: to move, be moving."

Brihat is vast (the root *bri-* means to grow) and is the key word to describe the triune nature of the Supermind, the *satyam-ritam-brihat*. It is the all-encompassing wideness which is one with the Truth of the Universe.

Satyam is Truth, that which is eternal, universal, and infinite. *Sat* is that which is *nitya* or unchanging and the Real. It is indestructible and holds the Universe together in its unity.

Satyam-ritam-brihat is the dynamic consciousness that connects the higher three *lokas* to the lower third. Sri Aurobindo calls it the Supermind and in his vision the next level of evolution on earth is when this higher principle manifests on earth in its fullest glory, transforming mind, life, and matter.

Amritam is immortality, the ambrosia of devas, the elixir of life. It is the *amritam* that transforms human existence to that even above the plane of the devas. The Vedic aspiration to become immortal is not just a vain seeking, but rooted in our spiritual truth and destiny. For in truth, we are children of Immortality, *amritasya putrah*.

Dhi is the inner seeing, or higher thought, later becoming a part of terms such as Buddhi, the pure intellect and mind. According to Sri Aurobindo, *dhi* represents thought. Elizarenkova shows how *dhi-* is another word that has perceptively been identified by Western commentators as having subtler meanings. *Dhi* according to Jan Gonda is an inner seeing, "to examine through an inner gaze" or as Louis Renou described, "voir par la pensée."

Dasyu is the dark force, the representative of evil and duality. The concept of the dark side of the Force is seen in all major religions such as Judaism, Christianity, and Islam. But in Veda, it is yet part of the essential Unity of *Sat* and the *Dasyus* are critical in humanity's evolution to a higher stage in universal harmony and brotherhood and consciousness.

Ekam Sat, One Truth, or *Tad Ekam*, That One, is the central insight of the Veda. That there is one Reality behind this multiplicity of the Universe. But the non-duality or Unity of Veda is not an abstract sterile concept, unlike the Monism of Spinoza. It is dynamic, alive, and multi-dimensional.

Vritra, the obstructor, blocks the mental energies to prevent the unification of the being of the seeker and let the knowledge be effective in the yogic transformation. It is he whom Indra the luminous mind destroys with his *vajra* or power of lightning to unclog the obstructed sea of light, *maho arnah*, of the heavens.

Nirukta means etymology. The original meaning of *nirukta* is that which has not been said, *ni + ukta*. According to the *Monier Williams Dictionary*, *Nirukta* is that which has been uttered, defined, spoken loudly, or explained. The only text on *Nirukta* we have from the ancient world is from Yaska which bears the same name. Swami Dayananda in our times emphasized the significance of *Nirukta* in his *Rig Veda Bhasha Bhashya* and used it to show how the Veda is a spiritual text which is monotheistic and holds many truths which we have forgotten. Sri Aurobindo with profound research in this Vedanga, and his scholarship in multiple ancient languages such as ancient Greek, Latin, and other European and Indian languages, showed its impact on what he called Embryonic Linguistics and Comparative Phonology.

Yoga means adding up or union. It is to add up all of one's divergent or disparate parts or constituents and make them all one. Subhash Kak in *The Idea of India: Bharat as a Civilisation* describes Yoga thus, "The practice that opens the doorway to intuition promised in the Veda is Yoga; they are the two sides of the same understanding."

युञ्जते मनं उत युञ्जते धियो विप्रा विप्रस्य बृहतो विपश्चितः । Rg Veda 5.81.1

The learned yoke the mind, also yoke the thoughts in wisdom's vast inspiration.

He describes the yogic processes in detail thus, "Holding the thoughts is dhyana. If one looks at the sequence of thoughts arising out of intuition (*paysan*, e.g., *Rig Veda* I.88.5c or X.124.3a) that through an intermediate stage is transformed to words, then the process of going back to that intuition is *vipasyana*." Vipassana, to remind the reader, is an ancient technique used by the Buddha to meditate and is still a major aspect of Buddhistic practices today.

Sutra literally means a thread or string. This is an ancient Indic genre where highly condensed wisdom is presented in prose or poetry. They may consist of rules, theorems, or aphorisms to establish the principles in the reader's or listener's mind with force, permanency, and concision. They are usually of a high literary quality and jump from thought to thought with an intuitive experienceable unity. We see these *sutras* for the first time in the *Brahmana* and Aranyaka sections of the Veda, which were both later additions to the *Rig Veda* to help explain and elucidate it for the initiates.

Subhash Kak has written 18 *sutras* in Sanskrit to present Vedic wisdom in a modern version of the genre. Some of these are excerpted here from his book *The Prajna Sutra: Aphorisms of Intuition*, to give the reader a taste of the age-old Indic literary form from another creative perspective:

The Sutras
Cidakasasya tadiyau surya-candrau
The inner sky has its own sun and moon.

Manasi pratibimbitam brahmandam
The universe is mirrored in the mind.

Samanya adharitam jnanam
Knowledge is based on the universal.

Sabdah bandhah
Word associations lead to paradox.

Bhasa apara
Linguistic knowledge is of limited kind.

Viruddhani iva api darsanani paraspara-purakani
Darsanas, although seemingly contradictory, are
complementary.

Bhasa-loka-viruddha-abhasa-atitam vijnanam
Vijnana is beyond language and paradox.

Yajnat prajna avirbhavati
Prajna emerges out of yajna.

Yajno yogah parinamah parivartanam ca
Yajna is yoga, which is becoming and transformation.

Recursion is a principle in mathematics and computer sciences
where the simplest base case is used to create a function that is
then endlessly repeated to create a set. The Veda uses the principle
of recursion or recurrence in an ingenious manner, according to
Subhash Kak in *The Idea of India: Bharat as a Civilisation*. Many
fractals are created using the recursive approach.

Appendix V: Glossary

Advaita: Literally, means no-two. The understanding that the Universe is one Reality, that each individual is secretly that Reality, and has the potential and the ability to experience and live that Reality.

Adhyatmik: Spiritual. Made of two words *Adhya-* and *Atmik-*. The highest interpretation of Veda, a tradition as old as Veda itself.

Adhi Bhautik: That which is physical. Ritualistic interpretation of Veda.

Adhi Daivik: That which pertains to the realm of Devas. Or a mythological interpretation of Veda.

Aditi: The mother of Devas. The Indivisible One.

Adri: Stone or hill in Veda. Signifies the Inconscient.

Agni: Fire. In Veda, represents Fire and Light of revelation. Agni implies that which is eminent, the leader, the organizer, the invoker, the purifier, our seer-will, divine love, the Atman, and the Paramatman. Cognate with the root of the word igneous. Thus, when we ignite a mind or heart, we are invoking Agni.

Akshara: Alphabet in Sanskrit.

Alankara: A figure of speech. Literally, an ornament.

Amritam: The state of immortality or the elixir that brings immortality by partaking it.

Ananda: Bliss. Another term used for it in Veda is Soma. *Ananda* is the origin of the Universe; it is its every movement and seeking, and it is its destination according to Vedanta.

Ananta Vartmana: The Eternal Present.

Angirasa: Vedic term for rishis who were our forefathers, born of Agni. Perhaps the earliest rishis of the Vedic lore.

Anukrama: Order.

Apaurusheya: That which was not created by any man.

Aparardha: Lower half of the Vedic model of the world, comprising matter, *prana*, and mind, or the three lower *lokas*.

Aradhya: The one who is worshipped.

Arya: A noble refined person according to Veda. Derived from the word ari-, which means to plow.

Arya Samaj: The Society of Arya that Swami Dayananda established.

Atman: The Self.

Beej Dhvani: Seed sound.

Bhadram: The auspiciousness, the good that comes out of living in the Self and performing *yajna* or yoga.

Bharata: The ancient Sanskrit name for India, among many other names for it.

Bhasha Vigyana: Linguistics.

Bhashya: Exegesis, critique, commentary, explanation. The ancient Indian tradition of explaining sacred and important texts.

Bhumi: Earth, ground.

Chhanda or Chhandic poetry: Form poetry.

Darshana: Literally, to behold. A term often erroneously translated into philosophy.

Darshanik: One who beholds the Truth.

Dasyu: Being of Darkness. Also called *Dasa*, born of duality, who opposes the rishi in the *yajna*.

Deva: Literally, a being of light. *Div-* means light, cognate with English word Diva.

Dharana: Focused and sustained consciousness.

Dharma: Literally, that which holds one together. The way of being.

Dhi: Refined thought or mind, according to Sri Aurobindo. The word Buddhi or elevated and refined mind comes from *dhi-*.

Dhyana: Meditation.

Dvaita: Duality. The dividing or separating principle that creates an existence that is disparate and disjointed from itself.

Ekam Sat: One Truth. Also known as *Tad Sat, Tad Ekam, Tad Adbhutam*.

Etad vai tat: This is That, one of the *Mahavakyas* or great sayings of Vedanta.

Fractal: The mathematician Mandelbrot defined a geometric fractal as "a rough or fragmented geometric shape that can be split into parts, each of which is (at least approximately) a reduced-size copy of the whole." They are characterized as having self-similarity, i.e., the part is similar to the whole either exactly or significantly. And they have an intricate pattern. Thus, the lungs might be said to be a fractal of a branching tree. Or the human being as the fractal of the Universe.

Gau: Ray of light or Divine Knowledge, according to Sri Aurobindo. The term has many other interpretations including cow, Aditi, night-sky, receptive mind, song, etc.

Gauri: Literally, the bright one. One of the forms of the Divine Mother.

Ghritam: Ghee or purified butter, literally. In Veda, it is a symbol for the clarified density of mind that is luminous with brightness.

Gomati: Literally, the river of light.

Gopuram: The sacred area at the entrance of a temple.

Guhya: Hidden from *Guha*, which means a cave.

Guna: Quality.

Gurukulam: An ancient institution where the students boarded and lived with the rishi and learnt from him or her for 7-14 years.

Hiranyagarbha: The Golden Womb which is the origin of the Universe in the *Hiranyagarbha Sukta*, a Creation Hymn in Veda.

Hota: One who invokes. Term used for Agni in the first mantra of the *Rig Veda*.

Hrdi: Heart.

Inconscient: Term used by Sri Aurobindo, signifying the greatest density of unconsciousness where there is no awareness or cognition at all. Equivalent term for it in Veda is *Salilam Apraketam*.

Indra: The deva of luminous mind, according to Sri Aurobindo.

Indriyan: Senses, which may be gross or subtle.

Indu: Another term for Soma or Bliss. Also means the moon.

Ishvara: God. The Divine who is the Lord of the Universe.

Jati: Translated usually as caste, but traditionally the social division was based on aptitude and skill, lineage of Guru or activities, or bloodlines.

Kaarana Shareera: The Causal Body that bears and upholds the Subtle and Gross Body of an individual or organization.

Kalasha: The container that holds Soma, usually refers to the heart that holds the bliss in its *dharana*.

Karmakanda: The interpretation that Veda is all ritual.

Kavi: The seer-poet. One who can see beyond and see through time, space, and causality, and express it in words that bear the vision and is able to transmit that vision.

Ketah: Intuition or revelation, according to Sri Aurobindo. Also means a comet. Thus, in the higher mind of the rishi, the blaze of intuition might remind the rishi of a comet.

Kriya: Action. Usually associated with Kriya Yoga, where a physiological transformation is effected by certain yogic processes and activities.

Kula: Lineage that could be based on bloodline or relationship to a Guru and his traditions.

Loka: World.

Maho Arnah: The Great Ocean of light above. Also called *upari samudra*.

Mandala: A design representing the cosmos used for meditation in Tantra and Buddhists sects. The Veda is organized into ten mandalas. Interestingly, Carl Gustav Jung painted mandalas and used them for his Analytic Psychology.

Mandapa: Altar for Vedic weddings; usually a raised structure with roof and supporting pillars.

Manishi: The Thinker, one with refined and elevated thought.

Mantra: The Ultimate and Inevitable accomplishment of poetry.

Martanda: Literally, the dead egg. The eighth child of Aditi, the Indivisible, the Mother of all devas, who was deposited in the Inconscient and the world of life and death, to emerge as a seed from the dense darkness.

Maya: To measure. That which we can measure is Maya. Another root of Maya may be Ma- or mother. Maya is the mode through which the Formless manifests into Form.

Mayas: In Veda, means bliss.

Mayavada: Illusionism or the doctrine that considers the world as illusion. Usually associated with Sankara, who may have been understood.

Mimansaks: Interpreters of Veda who consider it solely ritualistic.

Mitra: Means friend. The deva of harmony, love, friendship who is essential to the emotional growth of the yogi or seeker.

Monism: The philosophy that all existence is in reality one. Vedic monism is the realization of the Oneness of the Universe which allows for illimitable multiplicity and is not contradicted by the variety in its manifestations.

Monotheism: The doctrine that there is one God. Vedic monotheism is a dynamic understanding of the One God who has no other and is Lord, *Ishvara*, of the entire existence.

Mool Dhvani: Root sound.

Namakarana: The ceremony of naming a child in the Indian tradition, done according to certain processes of meditation and *dhyana*.

Narabali: Human sacrifice. It does not occur anywhere in the Veda.

Nastika traditions: Those who do not believe in the authority of the Veda, e.g., Jainism, Buddhism, Charavaka's materialism.

Nirukta: Literally, that which is said. It is one of the six Vedangas that focuses on the roots or etymology of each word.

Pantha: A path.

Parama Vyoma: The Ultimate Space where the rishis saw and heard the *riks* or mantras of Veda.

Paramatman: The Supreme Self.

Parampara: Tradition.

Parardha: The Upper Half. The worlds of *sat, chit,* and *ananda* above the Supermind.

Para Vac: Literally, beyond speech. The supreme level of speech in Tantra.

Pitras: Forefathers.

Potri: The Purifier. A term used for Agni.

Prajapati: Lord of the people. Term used for the Divine who gives birth to the Universe.

Pramaana: Evidence, proof.

Pramiti: Knowledge gained or established by *pramaana* or proof.

Prana: The vital energy that moves everything in our life. Also known as Chi, *Ruh, Ruah,* anima, pneuma, *qi, mana, orenda, od,* etc., in other traditions.

Psychic: A term used by Sri Aurobindo as the Divine within us, immanent in matter, evolving through life and mind, towards the higher light. It is the Agni in our heart, forever burning, unstainable, indestructible, as the Divine *Tejas* within us, the seer-will, the *kavi* or poet, the Divine Love in our center.

Puranas: Indic texts that may be considered its mythology. The Puranas take their essential schema of the seven *lokas* from the Veda along with the trinity of Brahma-Vishnu-Shiva. But the Puranas are not *Sruti* or Revelation.

Purohit: One who is at the front; from the Sanskrit word *puratah*, which means the front. A term used for Agni in the first mantra of the *Rig Veda*.

Raga: The Indian melodic framework in classical music.

Rasa: Literally, the essence or extract. *Rasa* is the joy that comes from the touch of things in the world, and originates in the original bliss, the Soma or *ananda* that is the source of the Universe.

Recursion: Literally, recurrence or run back. In mathematics, it is a method by which a thing is defined in terms of its own component parts until a base case is reached. According to Subhash Kak, it is one of "the central insights of Veda."

Ribhus: "The first human beings or human faculties (who) became divine and immortal powers by perfection in their work," according to Sri Aurobindo.

Rik: Hymn of praise or worship. The word has two roots, *arc-*, which means light and *rik-*, which means song of praise.

Rishi: The one who creates the mantra or the Inevitable Word; who can see the vibrations or light of the mantra as it appears in his or her highest consciousness.

Ritam: Truth or sat in manifestation, according to Sri Aurobindo.

Ritasya Panthah: The Path of Truth.

Riten Ritam apihitam dhruvam: The Truth is covered by Truth, unmoving (*Rig Veda* V.62.1).

Ritu: The seasons. Derived from *ritam*, the cosmic law manifesting in the cycles of time.

Ritvik: One who has the ecstasy of Truth. Term used for Agni in the first mantra of the *Rig Veda*.

Sabda: The Sanskrit word for "word".

Sacchidananda or *sat-chit-ananda*: The trinity of *sat-chit-ananda*, or truth-consciousness-bliss, that according to Vedanta is the source of the Universe.

Sadhana: The intense discipline and spiritual practice of yoga.

Salilam: The Ocean.

Salilam Apraketam: The unmanifest Ocean usually used for the Unconscious or Inconscient basis of the Universe.

Samudra: The Ocean. That in which everything meets.

Sanatana: The Eternal, the Universal, the Infinite.

Sankhya: An Indian darshana or philosophy that posits two principles of the Universe: the Purusha or pure consciousness and Prakriti, the manifesting principle that creates the world.

Sannyasa: The renunciation of the world in post-Vedic Indic traditions. It means, literally, to let everything drop or to put everything down.

Sapta Loka: The seven worlds of Veda, comprising matter, vital, and mind below and *sat, chit,* and *ananda* above. Between them is the Supermind or *satyam-ritam-brihat*.

Sapta Sindhu: Seven Rivers

Sarama: Divine intuition, who assists Indra in discovering the rays of light or *Gau* hidden in *adri* or inconscience and helps him liberate them from the dark *bila* or cave. Represented by Western commentators as a bitch, which is an erroneous representation.

Sarasvati: Divine Inspiration and Voice who aids Indra in destroying *Vritra*, and helps him release Divine Knowledge and light symbolized by waters to come down to the lower worlds.

Sarvam khalvidam Brahma: All is the Brahman, another *Mahavakya* or master statements of Vedanta.

Sat: Truth or existence. That which is unchanging and may never be destroyed.

Sati Pratha: The tradition of widows immolating themselves on the pyres of their husband.

Sayana: Vedic scholar of 14th century who was a ritualist. Wrote the *Vedartha Prakash,* literally the light of the meaning of Veda. His greatest achievement is organizing the Veda as a document to be used by posterity.

Shlesha: Paronomasia or the pun (one word having multiple meanings).

Shunahshepa: Literally, the tail of a dog. A hymn compiled by rishi Shunahshepa himself that describes his mythologic symbolic journey of personal liberation and fulfilment in Veda.

Siddhi: A spiritual realization that is established in the yogi.

So hum: That I am, another *mahavakya*, or master statement, of Vedanta.

Soma: Bliss. Also means the moon. It is the bliss that arises in the being and body due to yoga.

Somarasa: The rasa or essence of Soma, the joy of drinking it.

Sookshma: The subtle. Cognized or sensed by subtle senses or consciousness.

Sookshma Shareera: The Subtle Body or Psycho-Physical discovered by yoga, which bears, supports, and envelops the Gross Body.

Sruti: Revelation. Literally, hearing.

Sthoola: Gross. The physical.

Sthoola Shareera: The gross body.

Stuti: Praise.

Sukta: Literally, well said. In the Veda, it stands for a collection of hymns on a particular deva or theme.

Supermind: The principle as described by Sri Aurobindo that creates the world. The equivalent term for it in Veda is *satyam-ritam-brihat*, the Truth, the Right, the Vast. Supermind is a dynamic globally unifying consciousness where the will is not apart from its execution, the word is not separate from the idea.

Surya: The Sun.

Sutra: Literally, a thread. An ancient genre of Indic civilization, formulae or keys to understand an issue or text, consisting of highly condensed statements of a principle or intuitive truth.

Svadharma or *Swadharma*: One's dharma or way of being.

Svarajya or *Swarajya*: Literally, self-rule or self-mastery.

Svasti: The goodness, benevolence, protection, happiness that comes out of the Self, *Sva-*.

Tad Adbhutam: That Mystery. Also used for *Tad Ekam* or *Tad Sat*.

Tad Ekam: That One, or the One Truth of the Universe.

Tad Sat: That Truth, the unifying Reality of the Cosmos.

Tantra: An ancient *marga* or path in Indian darshana that attempts to find liberation through worship and adoration of Shakti, the Active and Feminine Principle of the Universe, that executes all action and activities. Comprises three essential modes, the mantra, the yantra, and tantra.

Tapasya: Literally, heat, that comes into being with yoga or the fire of *yajna*, the Agni.

Tat tvam asi: That am I, another *Mahavakya* or master statements of Vedanta.

Tejas: The yogic energy that appears after *Tapasya*. Also, represented by Agni.

Ubhaya Alankara: A figure of speech that has two elements, one is the play of sounds or syllables and the other a play of meaning. For example, if a figure of speech were an alliteration and a *yamaka* at the same time, it would be *ubhaya*.

Vac: The goddess of Speech. May also mean speech itself.

Vaikhari: The fourth or outermost level of speech in Indian yoga where sound becomes audible.

Vala: The dark being who hides the rays of light or *gau* in the *bila* or cave in *adri* or the inconscient. Indra, with the help of Sarama and *Angirasas,* helps release this light from the darkness back to freedom.

Vani: Voice

Varuna: The deva of vastness, expanse, and the ocean. Varuna is closely associated with Mitra and together they are critical for the emotional growth and purification of the seeker or yogi.

Vayu: The deva of *prana* or vitality, usually taken as the deva of air.

Veda: Literally means knowledge. The Veda is the oldest document of Indian history that may be somewhere between 10,000 to 4,000 years old.

Vedi: Vedic altar.

Vedanga: Literally, a body of Veda. Usually, there are six Vedangas, which are specialized fields dedicated to study the Veda. These are *kalpa* (ritual), *jyotisha* (astrology), *siksa* (pronunciation and chanting), *nirukta* (etymology), *vyakarana* (grammar), and *chhanda* (prosody). We believe new ones may be added, including semiotics or the study of symbols, morphology, and, most importantly, *adhyatma* or spirituality.

Vedanta: One of the highest achievements of Indian darshana. It states that the whole Universe is one Reality, and each individual is an integral part of that Reality. And that everyone can experience that Reality and be one with it.

Vid-: To know, from the Sanskrit root that is cognate with the Latin video.

Vishisht Advaita: Or Special Advaita, Advaita with distinctions. Associated with Ramanuja (11–12th-century teacher and philosopher).

Vishvadeva: All gods, represented as one god who has all their powers, invoked in several mantras in the Veda.

Vishvakarma: The Designer of the Universe. Term used for the Creator of the world in two Creation Hymns in Mandala 10 of the *Rig Veda*.

Vishvaroopa Darshana: The revelation that Arjuna had when he beholds the Universal Form of Sri Krishna, in all his vastness and fearful appearance, in the 11th chapter of the Gita. Sri Aurobindo's experience of Narayana in Alipore Jail may be similarly called the direct experience of the Divine in everything and as the One and All.

Vritra: The dark being who obstructs Indra from bringing divine knowledge or light to the human mind, vital, and body. *Vritra* is often depicted as a snake which blocks the rivers of light flowing down; who is killed by Indra's *vajra* or thunderbolt to release the supramental waters into the lower world.

Vyakarana: Grammar

Yajna: An offering of self and all one's possessions to the Divine. Also means Vishnu, Shiva, yoga, and dharma.

Yamaka: A figure of speech in which a word repeated every time has a different meaning.

Yantra: A device with a design that has a force and effective power of manifestation due to its form.

Yuga: Term for an age in Sanskrit.

About the Author

Pariksith Singh, MD, is a passionate and acutely intelligent student and exponent of Hindu Dharma, and one who has been deeply engaged spiritually and intellectually with Sri Aurobindo and his Yoga for almost all his adult life. Singh is also the author of two other remarkably enlightening books on the Master and his works—*Sri Aurobindo and the Literary Renaissance of India* (2021) and *Sri Aurobindo and Philosophy* (2022). Singh's approach and writings are uniquely personal and not academic at all. His works, though of a commendable intellectual calibre, are suffused with bhakti-psychic devotion for the subject that he has chosen as his oeuvre: Sri Aurobindo himself.